Basics of Budgeting

*How to Effectively Manage Your Money
and Acquire Financial Literacy, so You
Can Stop Living Paycheck to Paycheck,
Pay Off Your Debt, and Start Enjoying Life*

Table of Contents

3

Do **NOT** continue reading before you check out this budgeting sheet … or you will regret it!

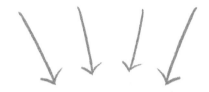

We highly suggest checking out this short sheet about basic budgeting first to become fully aware of where you are right now in the financial area before you dive into **Basics of Budgeting**.

>> **Click Here** to access this basic budgeting sheet to get the most value out of this book

Or type this link into your browser:

www.book-companion.com/basics-of-budgeting

Introduction

Money management is not something we are taught to internalize through formal education. We do not learn how to create a budget to pay our monthly bills, obtain the things we enjoy, or work toward having financial stability or security. We are left to sort out our financial responsibility ourselves. Maybe a few of us were lucky enough to have parents that allowed us to understand and properly manage money through our childhood and teenage years. However, it is more likely that you got an allowance and spent it on candy, toys or video games. When we grow up, we go through the excitement of getting our first apartment until the time comes to pay the rent and utilities. We experience the joy of starting a family, only to be stressed about how we will feed, clothe, and take care of our children as we work to barely make ends meet. We spend our lives working only to reach retirement and to realize that we only have a small amount in our retirement fund to survive our years of retirement.

Being financially responsible is not something one naturally possesses. It's rather a process of having to truly understand the flow of money, also called cash flow. For many, this simply means to pay the monthly bills we need to pay, leaving very little for us to enjoy. This is the case whether you are fresh out of high school, in your mid-30s, planning for your child's wedding or welcoming your first grandchild into the world. The problem so many of us face when it comes to our finances is that we simply do not know where to begin to sort out what we need to spend on and to keep it in balance with what we desire to spend on.

Millions of Americans are suffering through some form of a financial crisis. Some are trying to sort out how to afford a new water heater, others are panicking about sending their kids to college and most are simply tired of having to live paycheck to paycheck. They rarely truly enjoy or work towards the things that would give their lives a meaning. Ultimately, we shut down. We ignore the stress that we are feeling and we do our best to hide our disappointment and money struggles.

The truth is, staying silent and just hiding away from financial troubles is what causes so many to become anxious, overly stressed, depressed, and hopeless. It is what keeps us from living the life we truly dream of. Many of us dread going to work knowing that the paycheck we receive at the end of the week is not sufficient enough to meet our needs. Nevertheless, we continue in the same pattern of despair, dread, and resentment for all that we are lacking.

Money issues are one of the leading causes of divorce in America. Parents who constantly stress about how to pay the bills each month unknowingly transfer this fear of money onto their children, who then grow up to have the same struggles. An increasing number of individuals are living at or below the poverty level.This group does not only include young adults who may not know any better. Many individuals who spent their lives building a career and are close to retirement, lack sufficient funds to be able to live from during their retirement. They will probably be forced to get another job once they retire.

Wouldn't it be freeing to not have money control your life? What if you didn't have to worry about when the next paycheck was coming to pay the rent, electricity, water bills, or other financial obligations that you've acquired. For many, this seems like an impossible fairytale. So many of us have struggled for so long to gain control of our finances with little to no success. Maybe you have been able to pay off one debt, but in doing so you accumulated another? Maybe you are able to buy the things you want to but struggle to afford the things you need? Maybe you wish you could save for your first home, kid's college tuition, vacation, new car, or just want to have a safety fund set up for when life unexpectedly hits you with a financial curveball.

We all have these wishes and desires for what we want to do with our money, but just as quickly as it comes in, it goes out. Sometimes it is already spent before it gets deposited into our bank accounts. This never-ending cycle leaves us feeling hopeless, worn out, and disappointed.

I have been working with individuals for over ten years to help them gain the financial freedom they only used to dream about. I studied accounting and economics through college and worked as a financial advisor for some of the most successful businessmen and women of our time. I began my own financial advisory business to help others achieve the financial success that those of Fortune 500 companies have been able to achieve. These were people just like you, the Mom or Dad who wants to afford a better life for their kids. The fresh graduate that didn't know how to pay off student loan debt and be able to enjoy the hard work they had just completed. The first-time parents who wished they could buy a bigger home. They have been men and women who had been working at a job they had no passion for but couldn't find the money to pursue their dream job or start their businesses. These individuals are not unlike you

Throughout my work, I have guided individuals to financial independence. They not only have learned how to manage their money but have also learned how to make the income they are guaranteed each month to work for them. So many of the people I have worked with have been able to pay off debt, take vacations, set up retirement funds, tuition funds, make a down payment on their first home and much more. They didn't need to get a second job, work longer hours, or to take out unnecessary loans.

They were able to take an honest look at their income and their spending and to see the habits that were holding them back from living their life of their desires and not to live a life based on their financial constraints.

The one thing almost every client I have worked with has had in common is just not being fully aware or honest about what they were spending their money on. They didn't recognize how a little bit spent here and a little more spent there was adding up to a huge deficit in their ability to conquer their financial state.

I know personally how it feels to stress about what bill will get paid this month and what can be put off another month without having the water, heat, or electricity shut off. I was guilty of simply spending what I had when I had it. Growing up I was one of those kids who always wore clothes from my siblings, we shopped at Goodwill, and were kindly gifted other necessities from our local church. My parents fought constantly about the long hours my father worked and the little money my mom had to buy food for the week. I was not taught about money management or even knew it was a real issue. I grew up looking at money from a negative perspective. Secretly, I blamed the lack of money for my parents constant fighting and our constant state of not having enough and I feared that earning my own money would cause me to somehow fall into this unhealthy life.

When I grew up and was supporting myself, I had no idea how I would pay my rent and other bills, let alone be able to go out with friends, pay for my student loans, new clothes, a car, and much more. It became clear through my studies and my frivolous spending habits, that my relationship with my finances was a mess. I would sneak in and out of my apartment, praying my landlord wouldn't stop me to ask for the rent that was already a week late. I thought ignoring my lack of money would somehow make it sort out on its own.

I thought that once I graduated and started on my career, the financial strain would be lifted,yet it only got worse. I was falling deeper and deeper into debt with no shining light of hope that I would ever be able to recover from the hundreds of thousands of dollars of debt. Every time a new bill would come in, I would become physically ill. The thoughts of "how am I going to pay for this?" or "how can I afford that?" consumed me. I was living in a constant state of panic.

Meanwhile I knew my finances were a mess and I felt the stress of the strain every day, I didn't know how to solve the problem. It was much easier to tell those who had the money where they should be investing, but when you don't have that money it is not as clear to see what you should be doing. I didn't know where to begin. Should I pay off the credit card debt first? If I do so, how can I possibly put any money away for savings? Not knowing where to start kept me from doing anything about the mounds of bills piling up. It wasn't until I was forced to confront the crisis I had put myself in, I started the process of controlling my finances. When the crisis mode hit, my electricity had been shut off, I had let that bill go one too many months and to get it turned back on, I would not only have to pay what I owed but would also have to pay an additional $100. On top of that, I had gone home from work to find an eviction notice on my door. I had just 30 days to either get my financial crap together or get out.

It was one of the most stressful and anxiety-filled times of my life. In those 30 days, I had to get transparent about my spending and I had to get creative too. Once the panic had subsided, I sat down to reviewe my expenses and my income. By candlelight, mind you, I took it one week at a time and spent only what I had on hand. I made sure to set aside enough money so that at the end of the month the rent was paid in full along with the following month's as well. Then I made a plan to get my electricity turned back on. I used the same steps that you will learn through this book. First cutting out all non-essentials, going on a no-spend challenge, and giving every dollar I brought in a dedicated non-negotiable account. It took a great deal of discipline in those first two months but once I was able to get out of anxiety mode, it became clear that a budget would not only keep me from falling behind, but it would allow me to thoroughly enjoy the things I loved the most. I built up my money management confidence, made it a priority to become financially literate, and now even when those unexpected expenses come about, I am prepared and take care of them before they even have a chance to become a stress factor.

You don't have to wait until crisis mode hits. You don't have to wait until you are about to lose everything to take your finances under your control. In fact, it is possible for you to not only live a life that is free from money stress , but is a life that you have dreamt of. Furthermore, Regardless of how substantial or small your income is, it is possible to gain control of your finances and make your money work in a way that aligns with the life you aim to have.

This book is not designed to tell you what you can and cannot spend your money on. You want to buy a new wardrobe every month, have fun. You want to pay off your student loans in five years, consider it done. You want to take the vacation of a lifetime, it is possible. Many believe that in order to live the life they want; they need to be making more but in reality you just have to be more cautious about where the money you are making is going. Are you spending five bucks on a fancy coffee each day that you don't really need to enjoy? That equals $25-$35 a week which adds up to $100 or more dollars a month that you could be putting aside for what you really want in life.

These little impulsive spending habits are the number one reason so many people are unable to achieve the financial success they want in life. They simply do not understand or consider how these small purchases add up. One of the things you will learn through this book is how to identify these compulsive spending habits and correct them so you can save more.

We all have our own unique experience with money. Some of these experiences occurred at a young age and have been hindrances to our ability to remain in control of our money. Other experiences have discouraged us from thinking that we will never live up to our full potential. Others have caused us to neglect, avoid, or even consider that we can achieve so much more with just a little bit of understanding and effort.

"I grew up in a home that was never enough. There were five kids and there were never enough rooms, never enough space, never enough clothes, never enough food, and NEVER enough money. All my life

this has been a recurring theme. Just never enough. Never feeling like enough. Never accomplishing enough. And when it came to money, I never wanted to confront it. I had tried budgeting before, but every time I sat down all the bills added up and the income was never enough. I figured this was just the way life was meant to be. It was all I had known for so long and all that I knew. Until I started to actually track my expenses and uncover how much I actually had, I didn't think it was possible to ever have more than enough. Now, every day is filled with enough, and my income has been more than enough to pay off debt, buy a home of my own, and even allow for me to take a vacation once a year." - Daniella J. Age 34

"I have always had a steady income. My wife and children always have everything we had ever wanted. The bills were always paid on time, the kids got to participate in whatever interest they desired, and my wife was able to stay home to raise the kids instead of worrying about working. I had always thought that with my salary I'd be able to retire early and pursue other areas of interest. But, here I was at the age of 45 with no retirement plan and just a few short years to try to fund a substantial retirement fund that would allow me to retire in ten years. It was foolish of me not to begin planning and to start now seemed impossible. Two of my kids would also be heading to college in that time frame and we would have to find the money to pay for tuition and books. How could I possibly fund my retirement and two college educations at the same time? Going through the steps outlined in this book allowed me to

jump-start my retirement fund and college fund for the future. And I was able to do it without our family feeling deprived." - Jacob R. Age 46

"Money has always been a struggle. I'm a single mom working full time at just barely minimum wage. Sticking to a budget was impossible, I was always stuck in the fear of when the next paycheck would come, and that paycheck was always spent before it arrived. I never felt like I would ever be able to get ahead or provide for my children as I had desperately wanted to. I took on the no-spend challenge outlined in this book and honestly didn't think it would help much. We were already living a very minimal life so I didn't see where we could make any more cuts. It was a life-changing experience. For the entire month, I found new ways to spend less, save more, and gained the confidence to not only take control over my finances but to pursue a new, more fulfilling career." - Jessica B. Age 27

These individuals had the same mindset that you may have now. Someday I will start a retirement fund, college fund, get out of debt, be able to provide for my family. Someday I will buy my dream home. Someday I will remodel the kitchen. Someday I will take the kids to Disneyland. Someday I will be able to afford the life I dream of. They were all just dreaming of what they wanted without any clear understanding that they could be working towards and achieving their dream lives through a simple process. For many, someday was a fictional time period. It was a day that would never come but they stated someday to hold onto a little bit of hope that a miracle would happen.

However, someday is right now! Now is the time to change your mindset about the money you have. Now is the time to look at what your money can do for you. Now is the time to let go of financial stress and take control of where your money goes so you can move yourself from this life you are living to the life you love. And it all starts now!

Chapter 1: Basics of Budgeting

What we spend and what we earn are essentials for budgeting. What many people fail to understand is that knowing how much they need to spend each month compared to how much they bring in is a very generalized idea of how to handle their money. This covers the necessities for the most part, yet it doesn't take into account future plans, wants, or emergencies. If we only consider the bills we have to pay each month, we spend freely without ever obtaining the self-control to see what more we can do with our money. We impulse buy, binge shop, overspend, and charge regrettable things that we want to enjoy now. There is no planning for the future.

Why Create a Budget?

Budgeting is a concept, though foreign to most, that maps out how you can cover your monthly expenses with the income you have. For businesses, this is a crucial component that shows the profit or losses in their day-to-day activities and yearly efforts. It is what allows business owners to decide whether or not they can go all out on a new marketing campaign or where they need to cut back on unnecessary spending. It is what shows them where a majority of the money they bring in is coming from and where most of their money is being wasted. Even though you may not be a business, you can treat your life like one. Like a business does, you can use a budget to determine where you need to make cuts in order to increase productivity. It can be used to decide where you need to downsize and to improve in other areas. A budget is what will allow you to see where most of your money is going and if this is where your money needs to be going for you to expand.

A personal budget is about more than just determining where our money goes. When we create financial goals to pay off debt, save for a vacation, or put money aside for a new car or home remodel, we need to have a plan of how we are going to reach those financial goals. A budget will not only help you reach those goals. But also ensure that you are not spending money where you should be saving. A budget will help you to allocate exactly what you need to pay each month and what you can afford to spend elsewhere.

Creating a budget will ensure that you always have enough money on hand for the things you need and want each month. Many people shudder when they hear about budget. It is a natural reaction for those of us who have been struggling to afford the things we need while enjoying the things we want. A budget doesn't have to be a painful experience. In fact, creating a budget can not only be a fun process but will allow you to gain the confidence you need to be able to live the life of your dreams.

Imagine not having to stress about where money for rent/mortgage, utilities, car insurance will come from, or feeling regretful after taking advantage of a huge sale at your favorite store. Imagine not having to constantly say, "I don't have the money for that," "We can't afford it," or "Maybe next year we can get it". These phrases that have kept you stuck on a wheel of doubt and mediocracy can be erased from your vocabulary. Imagine having money to spend on vacations, retirement, college funds, home remodels, and everything else that you desire.

Learning to gain control over your money is the most effective way for you to not only afford the things you want, but to allow yourself to get out of debt and stay out of debt. The right budget will provide you with necessary steps to take so that you can easily pay off your debt without feeling like you are depriving yourself along the way. Your own personal budget will help you see the most important things for you and allow you to spend the right amount of money where you want to be spending it. You make the rules. A budget is something you create that fits with where you are right now in your life and helps you move to where you want to be on your own terms.

Debunking Myths about Budgeting

There are a number of reasons why people don't sit down and create a budget. Many of these come from not having a clear understanding of how a budget can help them improve their lives. For others, it is simply about not wanting to face the debt they've accumulated or confront their poor spending habits. The myths and misconceptions around budgeting are what will stop us from being able to move forward and really take control over our financial situations. No matter what age, income, or milestone you are at in your life, a budget will move you to the next level. In order to do that we need to address some of the most common myths you may be holding onto when it comes to creating a budget.

1. Not having the time to properly budget.

Creating a budget is not as time-consuming as many believe. Once the initial, starting tasks are accomplished, budgeting your expenses and income is a quick and painless process. You already know that half of your income is going to go towards your obligations. The remaining income will be dispersed into different savings accounts for future goals and money to spend for leisure throughout the month. If you keep your values in clear focus, then you will have few problems and will truly enjoy the process of budgeting.

2. Thinking you need to understand how to do challenging math.

Budgeting is straightforward. You start off with the money you have on hand and you just subtract what you need to pay out. Sometimes you may need to do a little bit of division to break up expenses that don't occur monthly into monthly payments. Anything else you need to calculate can be done with various finance tools or a calculator.

3. Budgeting is boring.

When you begin to see how much you can accomplish with your money, budgeting is anything but boring. When you begin to see the rewards of having a substantial lump of money leftover at the end of the month or you see your dream fund growing each month, you will be anything but bored.

Even when you are trying to save more, budgeting can be sort of a game and a fun challenge. Seeing where you can cut out here to increase there, will allow you to move out of your comfort zone. This is where your true financial skills will grow. Coming up with no-spend weekends/date nights, and other ways to limit spending to save for what is really important, leads to uncovering new interests that you may have never thought of before.

4. My budget is in my head.

This excuse is given by those who don't fully grasp what budgeting is all about. They think it is simply accounting for bills and income and not long-term goals and savings. A budget needs to be something that assigns all your income to specific accounts. Trying to track where your money goes in your head is only having a vague and uncertain idea of how a budget is meant to work. Assuring that you are spending and saving correctly every single month is not something one can possibly do and keep track of in their head.

Even if it was possible to track what you spend in your head, this is not a sensible way to create a budget to meet financial goals. In order to properly assess how much money you are spending in certain areas, you need to be able to look at and maintain accurate records of what you spend. Doing this in your head results in simply guessing and you won't be assigning all of your money to a permanent home. This leads to overspending on non-essentials and miscalculating the money you need to allocate for bills.

5. The only thing I need to track for an effective budget is what I spend.

Tracking your spending habits is only part of the budgeting equation. Tracking helps you look at your past habits, yet it doesn't help you make adjustments for the future. Your budget is the plan that you use for the upcoming month. Meanhhile tracking gives you an idea of what you typically spend in certain categories, it doesn't give you an idea of how much you should be spending.

A budget allows you to disperse your income accurately. It allows you to set limits and give yourself more freedom to spend on the things you want more of. Tacking lets you see where you can make cuts, but a realistic budget is a full plan on how you will use your money for the upcoming month, not just how you tend to spend. This way you can achieve the goals you want in your life.

6. I won't have any money to spend on the things I want by sticking to a budget.

A budget is what allows you to spend on the things you want. It also allows you to do this with less stress, guilt, and anxiety. When you create a budget, you are taking a realistic look at your financial situation and creating a plan that will move you to more freedom. Consider right now how much you regret buying certain things when you have a large amount of debt that isn't going away? Consider how anxious you become when a bill comes in and you don't have the money to pay for it? How much stress do you fight with when you know you have rent or a mortgage payment due? These may not be fun to spend on but when you learn to allocate your money to cover the things you need first, you have more joy when you can spend on the things you want without worry.

Sticking to a budget is what allows you to gain more confidence and control over your money. It is something you create with your own values and goals in mind. You make the rules. You set aside what you are comfortable with, pay off your debts, and work towards long-term goals, not just short-term satisfactions.

7. Why bother budgeting when there is always an unexpected expense to pay for?

Unexpected bills, setbacks, and money strains are going to occur. We all face them. As we have discussed and will discuss more in the final chapter, these unexpected expenses can be planned for. This is where budgeting can really allow you to prepare for these hard hits. When they occur, they won't feel as major and they won't drain all the money that you worked so hard for. Budgeting allows you to plan for any expenses and if you take the time to realistically look at where you are in your life, you will see that most of these 'unexpected' hits are not that unexpected which is what allows you to begin to plan for them in advance.

8. I don't have to worry about having a budget right now.

This is a common excuse used by those who are younger, or who don't fully understand how a budget can help them reach the success they desire in life. Many young adults think that they don't have to worry about living on a budget because many may still live at home with their parents or others don't have the number of expenses that most older adults have. However, a budget can be a great asset no matter what age or what your lifestyle may look like.

A budget helps you fund your future. Whether that is to pay off student loans, buy a car, take a vacation, or just stock your closet with designer shoes. A budget is what makes this possible. Most young adults feel that they don't need a budget because they don't have the debt or countless bills to pay for each month. They live off their credit cards, thinking that they can afford to buy what they want and worry about paying later. This is exactly how so many get trapped in a plethora of debt that they soon realize they have no way of paying back.

Before you get trapped by debt or feel you are lacking, a budget can allow you to set up funds to pay for things you may one day like to have. Maybe a new home isn't on your "need to have right" now list, but there's a good chance that at some point it might be, so why not start a small fund for it? Maybe you have dreams to travel the world and become a famous Vlogger; whatever it is you dream of; you will get there much faster with an effective plan in place. Your budget plays a key role in that plan.

9. Sticking to a budget means I will have to do things I don't want to do.

Not every aspect of budgeting is fun. Having to pay off credit card debt or set aside a chunk of your money each month, so you have the financial security in place when a crisis occurs doesn't sound like a good time. This is where your mindset-shift needs to take place. Budgeting is not about doing the things you don't want to do, it is about taking care of the things you need to take care of so you can actually enjoy the things you want.

If you are sitting on a huge lump of debt and you decide to go on a fun beach trip, there is a good chance that though you may be trying to enjoy yourself, deep down you are only thinking about how further behind this trip is putting you. You aren't really enjoying yourself because secretly you are stressing about what you'll have to face when you return.

Budgeting isn't about doing the things you don't want to do. You make the rules for your budget. You decide what you want to do. If paying off your debt isn't one of those concerns, while it is strongly encouraged that it should be, then don't put as much into paying it off. Budgeting allows you to realistically and honestly look at the rewards and consequences of your financial choices. Not paying off your debt doesn't help you achieve your long-term goals. No matter how much you try to defend the choice of not paying it off, lugging around debt will keep you stuck. You may not want to do it, but think of the freedom you will have once it is gone.

10. *I don't need a budget because I make enough money.*

Even those who make a substantial income need a budget. While you have more freedom with what you can do with your money, you still need to ensure that you are getting the most out of what you earn. Those who tend to get sucked into the "I make enough" trap, tend to not have anything saved for emergencies. They tend to just coast paying their bills. They don't have a plan in place for the future and often don't even consider what may occur if their income gets cut. Just as someone who makes not enough money needs to budget themselves, those with enough definitely need to do so.

Money In, Money Out

When we think of a budget most of us automatically think it is simply a way to see whether or not we have enough money to cover our bills for the month. While this is one component to budgeting, it should and can be so much more. Once the bills are covered, what happens to the rest of your money for the month? When you have an extra $20 in the bank where does it go? For most, it gets spent freely. We grab lunch, pick something up for the kids, or treat ourselves with that leftover money because we paid the bills so we should do what we want with the rest. What happens when you have an extra $100 or more left over? Chances are you do the same. You spend it without questioning where it could be going instead.

A budget allows you to have this same freedom with spending your money but does it with more intention. Your personal budget isn't just about covering the bills and then spending the leftover uncontrollably. It also helps you clearly look at what more you could be doing with your money.

A budget is a plan that helps you identify your expenses for the month, your income each month, and gives you a clear understanding of how you can make your money better work for you. It is an essential tool that will allow you to live the life you truly want. It helps you to exactly breakdown where your money goes and will help you identify where you want it to go.

This is not just a way for you to ensure that all your bills are paid and then doing whatever you want with the money left over. An effective budget gives every dollar you have coming in a job. You create a plan for what you spend on and where you save. This gives you complete control. Everyone's budget is different. And you get to make up the rules and guidelines for your own personal budget so that it fits perfectly with the lifestyle you want to obtain.

This takes away the worry of spending on things you aren't sure you should be spending on. It relieves you of the guilt of splurging because you aren't really splurging. You set money aside to spend on the things you enjoy. You make the choice that that is where your money will go.

When you create a budget, you break up your spending into specific expense categories. Each category will have an allocated amount of money to spend for that week or month. Each one of these expenses will be specifically named so that you immediately know what the money's for and will even motivate you to add more to the categories that bring up unpleasant feelings. This means you clearly identify where you want your money to go to. When you get specific about where your money is going, you can create an action plan that allows you to pay off debt, save for a vacation or not worry about paying all your bills for the month because they are already covered.

But this means that all your money goes to bills and debt repayment, which means you don't get to enjoy the things you really want. For many, a budget is unpleasant because they carry around a great deal of debt. They believe that they can't enjoy spending their money on other things until this debt is paid off in full and that could take years for many of us. This isn't the case, however. A budget is what allows you to create a plan that pays off your debt in the least amount of time while also being able to enjoy your hard-earned money. A budget helps you see exactly what you need to pay and also include in the other perks you want such as a vacation, spending money on clothes or dining out.

What a budget can help you see is where you are spending money frivolously. It will show you where you are impulsively spending money. When you begin to stick to a budget, you will notice so many of these impulse purchases are triggered by other factors. Many of us tend to spend emotionally or out of boredom. When you have a budget in place, you address these poor spending habits and adopt better ones because you have goals in place that you want to reach. This will help you to stop spending too much money and help you to save more.

How Will A Budget Help You with Your Money Problems?

If you are new to creating a budget it can be something you dabble with. It is hard to create a budget when you feel you won't have enough to cover everything you need to. A budget shouldn't make you feel stuck or hopeless. Instead, you should feel less stressed and will even be excited once you realize you can put money aside for the future and pay off your debt. With the right personal budget, you will:

- Gain a clear picture of your true expenses and income each month.

- Set and achieve financial goals.

- Stress and worry less about money issues.

- Plan for unexpected expenses.

- Be rewarded with more money freedom.

Before you sit down to divide and conquer your money issues you will need to take a serious look at what you want your life to look like. If you didn't have to stress about money, what are the things that would matter most to you? This is an important first step because understanding the "why" behind where you put your money will be what you look back to when you feel you are struggling or when you need to make an on-the-spot decision as to whether you spend or save.

If paying off your credit card debt is a top priority, ask yourself "why?". Maybe you don't want to feel the stress of having to pay a huge balance each month, maybe you want to be able to do other things with the money you are spending on paying off your debt, maybe you realized those interest rates are sucking your money right into a black hole.

If setting money aside for date nights or spa trips is a priority, why? Is it because you want to have the ability to connect with your partner kid-free? Is it because you want to have a day that you dedicate to your own personal self-care? What would having the money set aside feel like?

A budget helps you map out how you can achieve your money goals and reminds you of what you are saving for. By setting financial goals based on what matters most, you won't stress or feel deprived when you decide to save that leftover money at the end of the month instead of spending it.

No more stressful expenses

One of the goals of your budget is that it will allow you to reallocate money without stress when an emergency arises. There are plenty of things that suddenly come up that we don't budget for. The reason we often neglect budgeting for some of these things is that some of these expenses cannot be predicted. While we may not be able to predict when crises occur, we can be better prepared for them. A realistic budget will take into account those that seem to suddenly appear and make you feel without control over your money. Things like having to replace your car tires, buy a nice outfit for an upcoming wedding or unexpected medical bills. These things may occur suddenly and out of nowhere but if you truly think about this, they are not really unexpected costs. You know eventually you will need to shell out a chunk of money to cover some of these costs. Budgeting will allow you to set a little aside so that when the time comes you are covered. You won't have to worry about how you will pay for unexpected events because you will have already planned for them. These categories are not ones you have to contribute to every month. You can have a set amount that you would like to have set aside for certain unexpected curveballs and once that limit is met, you can distribute what you were adding to that account elsewhere.

Before you begin to dread having to add another account where you will just have money sitting there that you would much rather be spending, consider how you feel when these sudden money blows hit. If you are like most people you feel uneasy, anxious and incredibly stressed when these things come up. Keep in mind, it is more than likely that you will get hit with these little expenses throughout the month. One month you need to shell out money for birthday gifts, new windshield wipers and a vet bill. The next month, one of your kids broke their arm, the dryer stopped working and the dog chewed your only pair of nice heels. That month is followed by having to pay for summer camps, summer clothes and shoes once again because your oldest is growing like a weed. Each month there are a number of unexpected expenses that can keep you stuck. Nonetheless, if you honestly look at each of these expenses they aren't so unexpected. As you begin to work on a budget you can better track when certain expenses tend to come up more often. Maybe April is a month filled with birthdays, you know August will be a month of school shopping and November and December are going to require extra cash for gifts and holiday travel. You can begin to set a little aside each month so that you plan for these expenses. They won't feel unexpected and you won't feel stressed about having to dip into other accounts to cover the costs.

Get unstuck from credit card traps

With a budget, you stop spending what you don't have. When you are on a budget you only spend the money you have right now. You'll stop relying on credit cards to cover the things that your on-hand money does not cover. When you do use your credit card, you use it knowing that you have the money to pay off the balance in full. A credit card will be used the same way as your bank card is used instead of using it to spend money you don't have. You will only use it when you have the money set aside in your account to do so.

Improve spending habits

You can identify bad spending habits. When you start off on a budget you will track everything that you spend your money on. This includes those little impulse purchases of coffee in the morning, energy drinks when you fill-up the car with gas, that cute outfit you bought for little Abby because it was on sale. Every penny you spend will be accounted for and you will write it down so you can actually see where you are spending money unnecessarily. This exercise of tracking everything you spend is almost always an eye-opening exercise. So many people never realize that those small purchases add up to huge dollars that can easily be syphoned into a more useful account.

This isn't to say you can't spend on some of these little things every once in a while, nevertheless with a budget, you will assign a dollar amount to enjoy these little spending habits. This way, you are guilt-free about that gourmet coffee in the morning and may even enjoy it more, knowing that you made the conscious decision to set a little aside to enjoy that coffee.

What about fluctuating income?

Many individuals who do not get a fixed paycheck each week tend to think budgeting is impossible for them. Not knowing how much or when your next income is definitely going to arrive means you need a budget more so than others. A budget will allow you to properly allocate the money you have on hand now to cover your obligations and fund your desires. Those who do freelance work, sell their own products or simply have a job where hours change from week to week, so your pay also changes quickly to avoid budgeting.

Budgeting is not an easy task for anyone, but it is not impossible. Even if you are unsure of your next pay, you can still gain control of your money. Creating a budget is what can actually allow you to stress less about not having a guaranteed pay. It will allow you to relax and know that what you have on hand right now can be stretched to cover what needs to be paid right now.

Getting Started!

Throughout the next chapters, you will gain a complete understanding of how to make a budget work for your life and the life you want to be living. Each of the following will be discussed in further detail but you can get started with them so you can be ahead of the game when it comes to sitting down and dividing up your money.

1. Track everything you spend your money on for at least two weeks. A month would be ideal but two weeks can give you an idea of where you are making impulse purchases.

2. List all the money you have coming in for that time frame. Even if it was your birthday and you got a nice gift of a few bucks, track it.

3. List all your obligations. What bills do you need to pay each month, when do they need to

be paid and how much are they? Anything that has an interest rate attached to it, make a note of what this rate is.

4. Don't forget to list obligations that don't occur monthly such as car insurance (depending on where you live), taxes, water, oil for heating and so on.

5. Make a list of your top priorities. What would you like your money to do for you? Don't fret about whether you can afford it or the time it will take to accomplish it. Once all your obligations have been covered, where would you like your money to go? What do you want to achieve?

6. Don't get overwhelmed. You don't have to have all the money to cover everything you want right now. You just need to understand what you want your money to do for you. Visualize what your life would be like if you were debt-free, able to take vacations or to start your own business. There is no limit on what you can list here, yet take the time to carefully think about the life you want to be living.

Chapter 2: Acquiring the Right Budgeting Mindset

What should you be doing with your money? What can you afford? These are the most common questions one asks when it comes to figuring out our financial situations. Unfortunately, these two questions are wrong to approach your money. These questions often lead us to create stories about our financial situations. We can cause ourselves to stress more over insignificant money issues or remain oblivious to issues that we have been avoiding. How we view money and our beliefs around our capabilities to handle money significantly impact our money management skills.

Your Mindset and Your Money

When you are struggling financially it is easy to fall into a lacking mindset, this, in turn, causes you to become careless with your money. When you are trying to gain control over your financial situation it can become tough at times. But having the right mindset will allow you to maintain confidence in your ability to bounce back and stay on track.

Your money mindset is your underlying beliefs about money. They are based on your own unique beliefs and attitude towards how money works for you and in the world around you. Some of us have a lacking mindset when it comes to money; even if we are earning more than enough, we are in a constant state of fear of not having enough. Others have a carefree mindset. This mindset leads them to believe that money will just always show up when they need it, so they spend recklessly. Your money mindset is how you look at the money you have and your understanding of how money works in the real world.

When we have the right money mindset:

- We feel confident about reaching financial goals.
- We are persistent in meeting financial goals.
- We enjoy what we have while working towards more of what we want.
- We control our money.

The wrong money mindset is what causes us to:

- Ignore our financial situation.
- Spend money we don't have.
- Spend money on things we don't want or need.

Our money mindset has been strengthened over time. The way our parents handled their money, the way our neighbors display their money or the view those around us have on money, will develop our money mindset. Our money mindset can be changed.

We can begin to look at money as a way to help us achieve and live the life we truly desire. We can let go of the fear of what others think or believe about money. When we change the mindset we have around money, we can begin to see the opportunities that open up and take control of our finances.

Money mindset and financial situations

Our money mindset can either make us feel confident or intimidated when it comes to taking a closer and honest look at our money situations. The way we look at being rich or being poor greatly affects our ability to be financially responsible. If we have a negative view on being rich, this could hinder our ability to reach financial goals. Having a view that those who are poor are more persistent, noble or inspiring will keep us in a state of never having enough money because we would rather be noble than greedy.

The wrong mindset around money will keep you from asking for help and finding a solution for your money issues. Having a limited mindset around money can make us feel as though the things we want will always be out of reach. We give up our dreams and desires because we never fully believe we are capable of reaching them. When we get hit with a financial blow, we are not only disheartened, but this strengthens the limiting belief that we are incapable of getting ahead.

Your relationship with money

Your mindset greatly affects the relationship you have with money. Many of us turn to spending as a way to feel better about ourselves or to comfort a disappointment. Emotional spending is a serious issue that can be keeping you from making any progress on your financial goals. When we begin to improve our relationship with money, we can begin to improve our money management skills. We can do this by first changing our lacking mindset and then evaluating where our money beliefs arise from.

1. *Changing your lacking mindset*

When you have a lacking mindset, you tend to think that your money is always scarce, no matter how much of it you actually have coming in. Adopting an abundance mindset allows you to embrace the money you have, the money you spend and the money you are able to save. With this type of mindset, we won't turn to spending as a way to make us feel like more. We won't feel the need to obtain more or feel the need to buy more to feel better about ourselves. An abundance mindset will help us remain genuinely happy even in times of disappointment and therefore we will refrain from the need to emotionally spend to fill a void.

2. *Evaluate where your money beliefs come from*

There are many instances from childhood that could have contributed to having a lacking mindset when it comes to money. As mentioned earlier in this chapter, not having enough money can make us believe that anything we want is always going to be out of our reach. Often, this belief stems from growing up in a situation where money was scarce. Maybe you never had the nicest clothes growing up. Maybe you never got to have a new toy because money was limited. This situation was out of your control, but it can have a huge impact on how you view money today. Never being able to have the same nice clothes as your peers could result in having a mindset of inadequacy today. Never being able to get the toy you dreamed of as a child can turn into a mindset that keeps you from believing your dreams are actually possible. The way we view money not only affects the way we spend or save, but also affects the way we simply live our lives. Take a moment to really evaluate your money mindset and then look closely at how you grew up. There is a fairly good chance that your outlook on money stems from your childhood. The good thing about identifying these limiting beliefs, that were based on your childhood, is that they can be reframed.

What occurred in your childhood was out of your control. This is important to remember since as an adult, your money is in your control. While you may not have been able to do all the things you wanted when you were a child, you can do them now. When you begin to reframe your beliefs and give yourself more power, you will be able to do more with your money.

Living Paycheck to Paycheck

Even those who make a decent income each year still struggle with saving money. No one is exempt from the unpleasantness of falling into the living paycheck-to-paycheck cycle. In fact, a majority of Americans are living paycheck to paycheck. In a recent survey, an astonishing 53% of participants said they lived paycheck to paycheck (Berger, 2020). On top of that 1 in 10 participants admitted that they couldn't even cover a week's worth of their essentials if they were not getting a paycheck and nearly 44% confirmed they wouldn't be able to pay for their housing if they missed just one paycheck that month. (Berger,2020).

This isn't just a scary thought; it is a reality for so many people. Even those who have a higher income are not exempt from paycheck to paycheck living. Having a higher income does not equate to less financial stress.

What does it mean to live paycheck to paycheck?

Living paycheck to paycheck doesn't mean you are not making enough money. Although individuals and families who make less money find it harder to get by, this doesn't mean you are stuck in a paycheck-to-paycheck financial strain. It means you are bringing in just enough to make it through the week. It means you are not saving, typically have a high amount of debt and rely on the next paycheck just to get by.

No matter what income you bring home each week, month, or year, if you are not putting anything away for savings, it is more likely that you will be living paycheck-to-paycheck. This means you are always paying for bills and other items that use up all of your pay for that time frame. You may not be spending everything on bills and your other financial obligations, but it means you are not setting any side for emergency savings or putting any money away for the things you really want to be able to afford.

This constant spending with no savings and nothing left over at the end of the week or month, makes us feel as though we are not making enough. It makes us feel as though we will be stuck in a dead-end job, run-

41

down apartment or unhappy living situation indefinitely.

There are many reasons why even those considered to be making a middle-class wage get trapped in a paycheck-to-paycheck arrangement. For these individuals, there are additional costs for going to work. Most middle-class wage earners have to worry about childcare, mortgages, transportation costs, their kid's extra activities, health care and more. These expenses make it almost impossible for those with a middle-class wage to save.

Nevertheless, more money doesn't mean you automatically have more to save. Instead, it means you have more to spend, saving is always an afterthought. It is always considered a "someday" goal. Those who are making more have a higher cost of living. These living expenses are looked at as necessities; there is not much thought going into where all this money is actually going.

Living paycheck to paycheck is an easy cycle to fall into. It allows you to simply spend money without looking closely at where all the money is going to. You may be thinking that you are stuck in this way of living. You may dread the thought of monthly bills coming in since that means your entire pay is going out. You constantly feel as though you will never make enough to stop living as though you are just getting by. While it is easy to live paycheck to paycheck, it is not a fun or fulfilling way to live. Constantly feeling stuck by your financial limitations makes it difficult to ever break free from this way of life. Living paycheck to paycheck doesn't allow you to focus on the things you really want or spend time doing the things you love. But this doesn't have to be your life.

Financial Discipline

To break free of the paycheck-to-paycheck living and to acquire the right money mindset, we need to strengthen our financial discipline. Discipline requires you to do the things you know you should or want to be doing even if you don't feel motivated to do them. Discipline can be applied to your money management by creating a budget and taking the necessary steps to achieve your financial goals. When you improve upon your financial discipline, you will be able to look at the short- and long-term goals that are possible for yourself. This discipline is vital when it comes to using your money for what is most important to you.

The discipline you exert to start and stick with an exercise routine is the same kind of discipline you need when gaining control over your finances. It is not always going to be easy or fun, but will reap the most rewards if you stay on track. There will be times when you will need to turn down a night of fun with friends or skip on by the newest smartphone but in the long term, having the discipline to say no to the instant gratification will result in reaching the goals that will make you happier for more than just a few days.

One needs to have discipline in order to sit down to create a budget. It takes discipline to admit you have financial struggles and be honest and committed to creating a plan to change your situation. Without discipline, it will be a challenge to stick with a budget that will give you the freedom you desire. We need to let go of this instant gratification for long-term success and happiness.

Beginner Budget Tips

No one wants to sit down to create a budget. The very thought of it can put someone to sleep or send them running for cover. The truth is so many of us do not create a budget because one: isn't very fun and two: requires us to actually look at what we are spending our money on. Also, not fun.

But if we can look at budgeting as a more eventful process that allows us to feel in control and optimistic, it can be a much more pleasant and even enjoyable activity. There are also a few ways creating a budget can be more fun.

1. Name your accounts

No this isn't just naming your accounts as an emergency fund account, college tuition account or retirement account. This is creating account names that will give you a chuckle or motivate you to add more to the account. Instead of an emergency fund name it "when sh*it hits the fan" account. Instead of a college tuition fund name it "little Abbey will do great things" fund. Giving your account fun and more personal names will give you a deeper connection and make the investment in these funds more meaningful.

44

You can do this with any credit card you have opened. We will go into greater detail about managing your debit/credit cards a little later. But, for now, you can label each of your cards for a specific purpose. If you know you will use one to pay off bills you can tape a piece of paper to it with "BILLS ONLY" label on it. This can stop you from using the card for any other purpose.

2. Create a visual

If you have kids, you know how effective a rewards or sticker chart can be. Yet, these aren't just for your kids. You can create a fun visual that motivates you to add more and helps you see your dream becoming a reality. You can make this visual as fun or as simple as possible. Use a square chart or a thermometer and fill in a square or an area of the thermometer each time you make a debt payment or add to your savings.

You can make it even more fun by drawing big bubble letters of the nickname you have given to your debt accounts. When you are making that progress on that debt, color a little bit of the letters with each payment until it is paid off. Whatever motivates you, use it. Don't worry about how crafty or creative you are, just find something that helps you see your progress on a daily basis and something you can celebrate.

3. Don't eliminate the occasional fancy coffee or new shoes

Instead of making these impulse purchases and then feeling guilty for spending on them, create an account in your budget that allows for the fancy coffee or shoes. It is ok to set a little aside for those special things you want to enjoy. If you know you have everything else covered and you have some cash leftover and don't know where it should go, place it in your fancy splurge fund.

4. Set a budgeting "date" with your money

You want to be checking in with your budget regularly. At first, this might be once a week when you are first tracking your expenses and getting used to only spending what you have. Then you may bump this date every two weeks to keep you on track. Whichever you decide, it is best to stick with at least one day where you review your income and expenses. Make this a top priority appointment but make it a fun one. Maybe you treat yourself to a nice lunch while you go over your money plans or spend a quiet evening with your favorite wine. Set a date with your budget, preferably a day when you have just gotten your paycheck and before you have spent any of that pay. Sit down and decide where your money from that pay is going that week or for the next two weeks. All you need is one hour every other week, but you need to strictly commit to this date as you would to any other major appointment.

Making the Right Decision on Spending Habits

Creating smarter spending habits doesn't mean you have to take all the fun out of spending your hard-earned money. When you make better spending choices, you will find that you can better enjoy what you are putting your money toward. When we carelessly spend our money, we frequently feel guilt or shame about what we have spent our money on. To avoid this vicious shame/guilt cycle, we need to develop better spending habits.

Spending money is going to happen, there is no way to avoid paying the bills you have to pay every month. You can ensure that you not only have enough to cover your monthly bills, but have enough money to save or spend on the things that are important to you. Creating a budget is the first step to developing better spending habits. Moreover, once you create your budget, you need to overcome the obstacles of impulse spending, emotional spending and spending too much money on the things you can get for a better price.

Spending wisely

So much of our money goes to things that we can easily avoid spending money on. Some of the most common places where you unintentionally spend more than you should include:

- Eating out
- Going over cell phone data/minutes
- Buying multiple items of things you already have
- Online shopping
- Buying things on sale

These are just a few ways we spend more than we need to. While it is very tempting to buy something that is on sale for a great price, do you necessarily need that item? Just because you have the opportunity to get something at a lower price doesn't mean you have to give in to the temptation to buy it.

In other instances, the opposite is true. When making a big-money purchase it is much better to hold off until you find the best possible deal or waiting until you know the item will go on sale.

Learning how to spend money more wisely begins by first acknowledging the bad spending habits we have and then finding a new way to replace those habits. Constantly buying things on sale just because they are on sale is a poor spending decision. Going out and immediately buying a high price tag item without doing the proper research or trying to find the best deal is another poor spending choice.

Additionally, we make plenty of poor choices with our money impulsively. What we need to do is become aware of these choices and find a better habit for them. For instance, if you find yourself constantly scrolling through Amazon before bed and making purchases on those Deals of the Day, instead read a book.

Another example can be reducing your risk of going over data or minutes on your phone by making it a point to check your usage. Set timers for how long you spend on your phone to limit how much data you are using. If you are at home, use your computer instead of your phone.

Good spending habits do not always come naturally. Many of us need a clear and solid incentive to develop these better spending habits. Creating small achievable goals is how you can begin to gain better control over your spending habits. Instead of grabbing lunch out five days a week, limit it to two or three days. Instead of grabbing a cup of coffee at the nearest coffee shop, make your own and take on the go. Instead of buying something as soon as you see it online, create a shopping list that you can add things to. This will give you something to save up towards as well.

Spending triggers

We all have our spending weaknesses. Maybe it is the smell of freshly baked pastries or gourmet coffee or maybe it's the big flashy signs that indicate there is something new from your favorite brand. Whatever it is, we are all guilty of having triggers that make us want to spend more than we should or want. Identifying these triggers can help you steer clear of trigger places that can throw you off your financial goals.

You won't have to avoid every bakery for the rest of your life. Once you have a better handle on how you spend your money and develop the discipline to resist the urge to spend on cue, these triggers won't affect you nearly as much.

Give yourself time

Impulse buying is the number one reason many get off track with their finances. They don't realize that spending a little here and there adds up to a huge amount by the end of the month. The best way to counter these impulses is to allow yourself an allotted amount of time before you buy. This can be highly effective for those who love to shop for clothes, shoes, kitchen gadgets or little things around the house. Set a time frame for how long you will wait before you buy that item. If after those days you still can't simply live without it, then go ahead and get it for yourself. Most often you may come to realize you do not actually want the item. Other times you may find that you can wait a little longer to buy.

Another way to gain control over your impulse buys is to designate a specific amount of money for those items you just can't live without. Allow yourself one day a week to indulge in those fancy coffees. This way you still give yourself permission to enjoy those things but have more control over how much you spend on them.

Increasing Your Financial Confidence

Financial confidence is the belief we have in our own ability to not only gain control over our financial situation, but to maintain that control. Many of us lack the confidence to make the best choices with our money. We fear that our past history of constant debt is how we will continue to live. We fear that we will always be putting our money in the wrong places and neglect paying off what we truly need and want to pay for. For us to be more confident in our ability to manage our money, we need to have proof to support this notion. To do this we can take small steps that can have a positive impact on our finances now.

1. Pay off just one small debt quickly

Look at all your credit card debt or bills you are trying to pay off. Are there any that have a low balance of 100 or 200 dollars? What do you need to do to have this paid off by the end of the month or by next month? Paying off just one small debt can give you a serious confidence boost and this can motivate you to pay off the rest of your debts in no time at all. Most of the time we look at this small balance and think about how terrible we are with our money that we can't even pay off this small amount. If we prove ourselves wrong and just pay it off, we increase our confidence and begin to gain more control over our financial situation.

2. Save $100 dollars in a month

That's just $25 dollars a week. Maybe you only indulge in your morning coffee a few times a week, take your lunch instead of buying a few times a week, maybe you skip on one of those sales at your favorite store and you make a meal from scratch instead of buying something premade or from the drive-in line. There are a number of little things you can cut back on for a short time that will allow you to boost your financial confidence.

3. Having $1000 in savings

Once you see how quickly you can save $100 dollars, challenge yourself to save up to $1000. If you continue to cut out a little unnecessary spending, you will have $100 each month to put towards that $1000, in ten months you will have achieved your goal. If you take it a step further and do a no-spend challenge, which will be discussed in further detail in Chapter 7, you can add this saved money to your $1000 goal and end up reaching it in half the time.

4. Set one long-term financial goal and commit to it fully

If you have done any of the previous exercises you should have a decent amount of confidence in your money management skills, which is what you will need when you begin to set long-term financial goals. Many avoid setting these long-term goals because of the time it will take to achieve them. On the other hand, when you begin to slowly work towards these goals, you gain more and more confidence. Decide on one long-term goal and start taking action to achieve that goal. This can be paying off all your debt, having an emergency fund that covers six months of your expenses or having an account that allows you to go into business for yourself.

5. Review your budget

If you have been sticking with a budget, that itself should give you a huge boost of confidence. However, are you really feeling confident or do you find yourself getting a little anxious before your next paycheck comes in? If you feel a little anxious, you need to do a check-in with your budget. There is most likely something that you are avoiding or neglecting. Maybe you have miscalculated your expenses in one area and that is what is causing you to stress before your paycheck hits. Maybe you are spending too much when you should be saving and this overspending is throwing off your budget. Having financial confidence is not just about sticking to a budget and savings. It also requires being aware of when you need to make some adjustments. By reviewing your budget when it isn't going as planned, you can build confidence in knowing that you have enough sense to rework what is not working instead of just giving up.

Chapter 3: How to Acquire Financial Literacy and Why it Will Help You

Being able to simply pay your bills each month is only half of the equation for gaining control over your financial situation. For most people, being able to pay bills each month is a paycheck-to-paycheck accomplishment. They are always planning on future money to come in to cover the expenses they need to just survive. Many of us approach our money with this survival mindset. Yet, when you are able to clearly understand and develop an effective strategy to pay your bills on time, without stress, without waiting for the next paycheck to come and without feeling guilty for spending money on the thing you enjoy, you will experience financial freedom.

The problem many of us have is not that sticking to a budget is hard or feels restrictive, it is the simple fact that we don't have a basic understanding of what our financial situation is and how to gain a better handle on the money we have right now. Becoming financially independent requires a number of skills and techniques that will allow us to implement the best practices for how to handle our money.

What is Financial Literacy?

Financial literacy refers to the skills and techniques that anyone can acquire to gain control over their finances. It is not that some people are just naturally good with money, they have had to take the time to learn the specific skills that are often not taught in traditional ways. These set of skills need to be strengthened just as you would strengthen any other skills you have mastered throughout your life. While financial literacy doesn't come naturally, it is something that can be learned no matter how old you are or what your income is. Individuals who are financially literate have a clear understanding of these three key financial factors:

1. *Budgeting*

Knowing how to create and follow a budget is one of the most crucial skills for financial literacy. As mentioned, creating a budget is not just about seeing where your money goes; it is about creating a plan that allows you to cover your monthly expenses and plan for the future. With a clear budget, you can have more peace of mind and feel confident in your money management skills.

Budgeting allows you to see exactly what you can afford to spend each month by designating specific financial goals for each area you want to contribute to. When you are financially literate you understand that delaying the instant gratification for buying what you want now will be much more beneficial for you to meet your true money goals. Creating a budget is something that does not feel daunting but is an effective way for individuals to see and become more aware of what they really desire. They use this budget to fund their current lifestyle while also working towards funding the future life they had only dreamt of before. Sticking with a budget is what allows them to turn their dream into reality.

2. *Emergency funds*

An emergency fund is one that covers all monthly expenses. This total should equal about three months of expenses. But three months of covered bills doesn't go a long way if you are out of work, facing a serious illness or injury or have another sudden blow to your ability to bring in a substantial income. Nowadays, it is safer to have an emergency fund that can cover at least six months of your total expenses.

When you increase your financial literacy, you will see how quickly and easily you can begin to build an emergency fund and grow it to cover your monthly expenses for up to six months. This emergency fund gives individuals peace of mind when their income gets tight or they are worried about the security of their job.

An emergency fund is essential to cover any big financial setback that we don't see coming. By preparing for them you will be less stressed and overwhelmed when these sudden unexpected curveballs come about. The financially literate do not just have an emergency fund, it is looked at as a crucial component to their overall financial goals. This emergency fund is what allows them to relax and stress less about funding all their other desires. Having a clear sense that they can make bigger plans because they have a nice cushion to support them if anything were to go wrong, is why those with financial literacy achieve greater success.

3. Debt

Half of our monthly income is spent on paying off debts. Credit card bills, student loans, mortgages, car repayments and other debts are what make it feel as though gaining control over your financial situation is impossible. One of the top priorities for those who have financial literacy is to pay off their debts as quickly as possible.

They learn which debt needs to be paid off first and which ones they can slowly pay off over time. They understand that as long as they have a significant amount of debt, they arc unable to fully fund the future life they desire. Financial literacy takes into consideration that time and money are wasted on paying off debt and this significantly impairs our ability to save or invest in our future.

Maybe you accumulated a great deal of debt in your 20s that in your 30s you are still paying off. This is often the case since most individuals are never taught that using credit cards to pay for the things they want now, without having the money, is a direct path to years of financial strain. Once we gain this understanding that these debts significantly impact our ability to save, then our money will work for us in the way we want it to. Taking the steps to get yourself rid of debt will allow you to make much more progress with your financial goals.

Becoming More Financially Literate

Financial literacy is a skill that can be strengthened and will allow you to gain a better handle over your money. It is what will allow you to save for the future and avoid unnecessary financial stress and strains. Financial literacy is what will allow you to fully understand how to create a budget that works toward reaching your financial goals. It is what will allow you to learn how to save more and spend less. Through financial literacy, you will learn how to borrow money and have a repayment plan already in place when you need to make big money purchases like a new home, car or college tuition. It is what will help you invest your money in the best way, so you get more return.

If you truly want to feel in control of your money, you will make it a habit to become more financially literate. You will be eager to understand how you can make your hard-earned money give back to you in multiple ways. You have more confidence in your ability to reach the goals you have set and to look at your money from a new perspective.

Becoming more financially literate will help you understand exactly what financial struggles have been holding you back. When you have a better understanding of how debt is holding your back, impulse buying is keeping you stuck or unaccounted for expenses cause you more stress, you will learn to manage the money you have with more awareness and purpose.

Financial literacy really highlights the importance of making your money work for you. You won't become discouraged by how little you have to set aside for savings right now, especially if that little amount is after you have made a significant dent to your debt. This is what allows you to understand that saving a little now is more important than not saving at all.

Make it a habit to learn about financial literacy. Most individuals lack the basic understanding of how to create and stick to a budget, but even those who have a clear understanding of how to budget themselves lack other financial literacy components. They fail to understand how to create a plan to really pay off their debt quickly, they don't allocate their money in the best places to account for "unexpected" expenses and they put off saving until everything else has been covered. Additionally, there are a number of things that you can learn to increase your financial literacy which will allow you to better understand how to manage your money.

Knowing the difference between a debit and credit cards, paying taxes, different insurance policies or how to set up a retirement fund, are all components of financial literacy that many lack.

Hold yourself accountable for your savings and spending. If you know you have big goals for your future but instead of setting aside, you are spending on dining out or expanding your wardrobe, you are lacking the financial literacy and accountability that will get you to where you want to go. Hold yourself accountable for where you are in your financial planning and future.

In the following chapters, you will learn how you can easily increase your financial literacy, nonetheless this shouldn't be where you stop. Gaining as much information as possible on personal financing is key to setting yourself up for future financial success.

Chapter 4: Becoming Aware of Your Financial Situation

There are many things that impact how we spend our money. For many of us we are unaware of what we spend on. We are oblivious to how much we are spending on little things and we feel that if we don't have what Sally down the street has, then we are not living a fulfilling life.

One of our biggest setbacks when it comes to managing our money is comparing our lifestyles with those around us or those we see on social media. We feel the need to have the next big thing just to keep up. This need to "keep up with Joneses" is a challenge we need to overcome. This is where knowing why you are spending your money and what you are spending it on needs to come into focus. Maybe Sally down the street has the new car but has nothing in savings, if a life event were to occur, she'd never be able to bounce back from the hit nor would she be able to keep up with the payments on that new car.

Additionally, we tend to feel more guilt when we see our family and friends spending money on things that we think we should be spending on. Your sister and her small family just got back from a week-long beach vacation. Your co-worker just invested in stock options. Your parents keep telling you to put more away for retirement and your kids are growing up so quickly that you feel you are way behind setting up a college fund.

In moments like these, where we begin to question if we are putting our money where we should, we need to take a closer look at our budget. Maybe you have been doing a great job at sticking with the budget you first created but are uncertain if you are making a great deal of progress, maybe you realized you want to be putting more into different saving accounts and maybe you had an "ah ha!" moment where you realize that some of the things you thought were important to you were actually only important because you have been comparing your life to those around you.

It is time to break free of the habits that can be affecting your ability to reach the goals that matter most to you.

True Spending Habits

In the first chapter, we covered why it is important to track every dollar you have going out. This tracking reveals what your spending habits are and allows you to have a clear focus on where you can be cutting out expenses that don't align with the goals you set. When you are honest about your money issues you can begin to change your habits and identify which ones are hindering or helping you. How you make your money work for you is the key to understanding and revealing your purpose in life.

Many find that spending on the latest fashion trends helps them feel better about themselves, yet this doesn't help them have the confidence to truly tackle the big goals they want to achieve. They may have the clothes to look the part, but their inaction keeps them from actually achieving the goal. Some find that giving to charitable causes makes them feel better about themselves but realize a small donation is only one way they can give back and decide that giving more of their time to volunteering is more beneficial. We can still spend on the things that make us feel good, however we often come to the realization that most of the money we are spending to feel better can be set aside for other things and we can have a bigger impact achieving the things that will really make us feel alive if we approach them differently.

Our good and not so good spending habits.

Our spending patterns can reveal specific lessons needed to be learned to gain control of our money. It is one thing to continuously impulse buy and identify these impulse purchases, it is another thing to understand why we feel the urge to spend. These patterns can allow us to understand what is truly motivating our habits and when we begin to uncover them, we can begin to make the necessary changes to stop or reduce how much we are spending on things that do not align with our overall goals.

Values are a key component to how we spend our money. When we begin to notice our spending patterns, we will also notice that we spend more on certain things because of the value we place at a higher importance. Maybe you grew up being told to look your best and therefore tend to spend more money on nicer clothes and more on keeping up your appearance. For many of us, our childhood greatly impacts how we spend and save our money. The thing about these values that we've adhered to since childhood is that they often don't align with what really matters most to us now. For so long we have just made it a habit to stay in line with these childhood values. We have never questioned or challenged whether these values have a place in our lives now.

Listing what you value most in your life will help you determine if your spending supports those values. It can also help you realize that while you may be spending on things that you find important; you aren't actually fulfilling what you value. For instance, maybe your top value is to spend quality time with your children. You make it a point to take them out at least once a week for fun dinner, maybe to the movies or to buy a new toy for you all to play with at home. While spending money on quality time with your children seems justifiable, taking a closer look can reveal that all the money spent doesn't have to be. You can get more quality time with your children by making a fun meal at home which they can help plan and make. Instead of going to the movies you can make a night of watching movies at home. Instead of buying a new toy you can sit down and do an arts and craft project with the things you already have in your home. By re-evaluating these core values, you can see where that extra money spent on family time can now be moved to a vacation fund.

We are creatures of habit and this is true of our spending as well. We tend to make repetitive spending choices whether it is the things we buy or the triggers causing us to buy instead of to save. We spend a great deal of money based on our value systems, especially the way we view ourselves. What we are willing to spend money on to improve ourselves and advance to what we truly want out of life. This can cause us to spend on quick-fix solutions.

Begin to understand your self-sabotaging habits. These habits include our attitudes, beliefs, emotional connections, and actions that contribute to our financial situation. Many times what holds us back from saving is a fear of not having enough. Many of us look at having money as a selfish act. Saving money instead of spending means we are only thinking about ourselves when we could be spending on others. This is where shifting our mindset can help us overcome our self-sabotaging habits. Feeling as though we are selfish for wanting more in our life is based on a belief system that we always need to put ourselves last. The truth is, we all want more and there is nothing wrong with this when it is done through hard work and effort. Begin to accept that when you are able to reach your financial goals you can benefit so many others along the way. Remaining stuck in your money struggles benefits no one, especially not yourself or your family.

Tracking Expenses

Spending frivolously has been made easier than ever with quick, convenient, and carefree shopping options. Years ago, you would have to track your spending by using a checkbook. But since we can easily access our accounts online any time, we place much less attention on staying on top of how much money is going out of our accounts.

The first place to start when tracking expenses is to look at these past bank or credit card statements. Checking your past accounts statement can give you a general idea of your spending habits. This will also allow you to see exactly what you have on hand now to spend and pay for the things you need right now. By checking your past statements, it is likely that subscription fees or services that you don't need, or use will stand out. You can easily cancel these things now so you have more money later. Nevertheless, you can't rely just on the last statement. You need to see what you are spending on a day-to-day basis and begin to recognize spending patterns that you can cut out.

We should already be tracking where our money is going. If this isn't being done there are a number of ways you can do this. Having something on hand that allows you to quickly make a note of where and what you spent your money is the most effective way to ensure you don't miss anything. Carry a small notebook with you or use your phone to create a simple note or spreadsheet that allows you to access it easily from anywhere.

After you have tracked your expenses for a week you can begin to make expense categories. These will consist of fixed and variable expenses. Fixed expenses are those that tend to be reoccurring and are typically the same amount each month such as rent or mortgage payments. Variable expenses will be those that tend to reoccur but can and often do change month to month such as food, gas, and household necessities.

By dividing your expenses first into fixed and variable expenses, you will then see what you have an obligation to pay each month and what your non-essentials are. Don't get discouraged when you notice what your actual obligation adds up to, or when you realize how much you are simply spending in the wrong places. This is what budgeting is all about. Becoming more aware of where you need to be spending your money versus what you actually are spending your money on. Tracking where your money goes is the only way to gain this clarity on what you are actually doing with your money.

When you are not making the effort to track your spending, you lose sight of what amount you actually have. You may think you have just enough to cover your bills or expenses but then find that one extra trip through the drive-in puts you over your monthly spending limit. Tracking your expenses also makes it possible for you to lower your bigger monthly expenses. Do you really need Netflix, Hulu, an all-inclusive cable package? Do you really need unlimited everything on your phone plan? Are there ways you can be more mindful of the lights on in the house? Lowering some of your major monthly bills can get you on the right track with your finances.

Tracking Your Full Income

Now you are aware of where your money is going, but what about where your money is coming from? Having a clear understanding of how much money you have coming in results in a more realistic budget that you can actually stick to. Don't get caught up in future money. Those with a recurring income, that is often unchanged, can easily determine what their income looks like. But there are often the occasional surprise income sources. These can include:

- Money gifts

- Rebates

- Refunds

- Side income or second income

- Selling items

Know everything that goes into your wallet and bank.

Here is where things get fun and interesting when you begin with a budget. While you may know how much you are guaranteed to bring in each month, this doesn't help you plan for when you need to spend more on bills and cut back on non-essentials for the week. There is a good chance that you have bills to pay throughout the month, they don't all just show up on the first day of the month.

When it comes to paying for your essentials, you want to only consider the money you have right now. Before you begin budgeting for a full month, you need to learn how to simply budget for the week without relying on future money. Future money is what many of us rely on and is the type of mindset that holds us back. We constantly think we can add more money to a savings account on the next pay or repay what we spend out of one account with the next check, but what happens when that next pay or check doesn't come or you had to miss a few days of work and isn't as much as you had planned? This is what happens when we get caught up spending money we don't have.

Determining Your Financial Situation

Are you financially healthy? Just as you keep track of your physical and mental health, your money should carry the same amount of concern. Financial health refers to your financial situation. There are many ways you can calculate your financial health.

Understanding your net worth can give you an understanding of how your financial situation has changed over time. Your net worth is essentially your assets minus your liabilities. Meaning everything that you currently own fully, compared to what you still owe or your debts. Determining your net worth can help you see exactly where you may be spending too much, yet this is more of a financial report card. It can be helpful to view this occasionally to see the progress you are making and to create a better plan for your future spending.

Your debt-to-income ratio is what most lenders will calculate to determine if you are able to pay back loans you want to borrow. This takes into consideration all your current monthly debt divided by your gross income. This leaves you with a percentage of how much debt you have compared to your income, before taxes. The higher this percentage the more negatively lenders will view your financial standing. If you are planning to buy a new home, this percentage is vital for being able to take out a mortgage.

While these two calculations are a good start to understanding your financial health, these won't necessarily mean much when it comes to creating an effective monthly schedule. Instead, you want to calculate your income to expenses. More simply put, are you spending less than you are making? When you have lower expenses, you are able to put more towards your financial goals. We've discussed the zero-balance budget. This type of planning assigns every dollar you have coming in a proper category. At the end of the month, you have no money left over but this doesn't mean you are just paying to survive. A zero-balance budget means you are funding your needs and wants each month. This includes putting away money for savings as well as working towards your financial goals. Every dollar is accounted for. It doesn't mean you have no money; it simply means all your money has gone to where it needs to be, so that you can live the life you want.

Do **NOT** continue reading before you check out
this budgeting sheet ... or you will regret it!

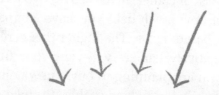

We highly suggest checking out this short sheet
about basic budgeting first to become fully aware
of where you are right now in the financial area
before you dive into **Basics of Budgeting**.

>> **Click Here** to access this basic budgeting
sheet to get the most value out of this book

Or type this link into your browser:

www.book-companion.com/basics-of-budgeting

Chapter 5: Put Your Knowledge Into Practice

Up until now we have discussed a number of topics that have led to poor spending decisions and why budgeting may not have worked out before. We dove into the myths and misconceptions that most of us think about what a budget is and what it is supposed to look at. We have tackled mindset issues that have kept us stuck in scarcity and addressed the habits that result in overspending. All these items impact the way we create a budget. If we don't first understand what a budget is supposed to be, we will never learn how to create an effective one. If we don't take an honest look at where our money is going to and coming from, we will never see the abundance we potentially have. And if we do not dig deeper into the limiting beliefs we have around what our money can do for us, we will never benefit from all we are able to achieve.

We have revealed a great deal of information up until now. All of the knowledge you will put to use to set up your financial goals. These are the goals that will allow you to bring the life you always dreamed of having into reality. Now it is time to tackle the issues we tend to run into when we create our budget and how you can avoid some pitfalls and stay on track.

Setting Up Financial Goals

Financial goals are designed to help you achieve what you want out of life. There are no wrong or right ways to set your goals, though there are more effective ways to establish which goals to set and work toward first. These goals can be short or long term and the duration of these goals will help you create an effective action plan that will lead to eventual success.

Long-term goals vs. short-term goals.

Short-term goals are those that can be achieved quickly, usually in less than a year. Short-term goals are ideal for paying off credit card debt, creating an emergency fund, holiday spending fund, or for minor home improvements or house decor.

Long-term goals are those that will take more discipline to achieve. These financial goals can take up to five years or longer to accomplish. This includes in-depth investing plans such as adding to a retirement fund, paying off the mortgage for your house, or saving for a new home.

Being able to set realistic short and long-term goals will allow you to create a feasible budget that will help you move towards your long term goals while still achieving each of your short term goals. Carefully consider what is important to you. What will bring you the most joy in life. This doesn't have to just stop at paying off your debt. Go further. What would your future life look like if you gained control over your financial situation now?

Budgeting Traps

Budgeting traps can stem from our misconception of what a budget is and how to properly use one. Many of us may have already fallen victim to these traps or have used them as an excuse to be honest about our money management skills. These traps are what will hinder us from setting short- or long-term goals. They will leave us in a state of lacking, not enough or wishful thinking that someday our money will just magically sort itself out. The most common traps include:

1. Not being realistic about your spending habits.

It can be easy to think you are not spending as much in one area as you think you are. This can cause you to remain in a state of denial. It is not uncommon for one to go through the month and not understand where the extra one or two hundred dollars they should have left over has gone. You already know where your money has been going if you have been keeping an accurate track of your spending. What you need to do now is be honest with how much you are comfortable with spending in each of your non-essential categories. If you know you love indulging in those specialty coffees, don't try to cut them out completely. You'll be setting yourself up for disappointment if you try to reel in the spending on every category all at once. Stick to changing one thing at a time, then move to the next. A budget should not make you feel guilty or ashamed of spending your money, it should rather make you feel in control, empowered and proud. The only way to make a budget work for you is if you honestly create one that suits you.

2. Paying off debt with your savings.

This can be very tempting. Many of us believe that if we can just get rid of our debt, we will be able to save faster. It is difficult not to use the money you have set aside for savings to use for paying off debt, but this can lead you into getting further behind. If an emergency were to occur where you need those savings, you would end up having to accumulate debt all over again. This can lead to becoming disheartened and never feeling as though you will ever break free of the constant debt cycle. While paying off debt can take some time, leaving yourself without an emergency fund can cause you to fall further behind. Calculating how much you can realistically set aside for savings while paying down your debt will lead to greater freedom. You won't feel stressed when emergencies or unexpected bills come about. When unexpected money comes in you can use this to pay off your debt further, although do not underestimate the importance of having an emergency fund.

3. Dispersing your money evenly.

It makes sense to spread out your extra income among multiple bills to help bring down the payments, however this is not always the most effective way to conquer your debt. Often this results in your payment barely decreasing. You may be spending more to pay off your debt, but it doesn't actually show or seem as though your bills are getting lower.

Creating an effective debt pay off plan will let you pay off one debt at a time. This doesn't always mean you pay the same on each debt. You want to be paying more on debts that have higher interests or that have higher end of the month balances. This will help you eliminate the debt that is hindering you the most.

4. Getting financing when you don't need it.

There are offers everywhere to get financing to help pay for big purchases. This is often how many get themselves stuck in a tunnel of debt. They get an offer where they won't have to worry about paying anything for the first 18 or so months and then suddenly those 18 months go by and you have nothing to pay. You are even further in debt and further away from your financial goals.

5. Getting too caught up with rewards.

So many credit cards and store cards offer nice perks when you use their card. This can cause you to want to use it even more often. While there is no shame in wanting to get more for your purchase, you don't want to fall victim to spending what you don't have. These rewards and perks are nice but the interest you pay on top of the purchase will often cancel out the perks. If you are going to use a card for the rewards, only use when you know you have the money on hand to pay off the balance in full.

6. Thinking you need to spend for others.

Keeping up with the Joneses as it is often referred to, makes you feel like you are either not doing enough with your money or spending it in ways that you shouldn't be spending it. This comes from comparing your life with what you see of others' lives. We feel we must have the same as our neighbors and we spend a great deal comparing what we don't have with what we see other people having. There are a number of problems with this view and allowing this to control how we spend or save our money. When you are constantly comparing how others are handling their money, you will never gain control over your own. Each person has different values that drive their spending, unlike many of these other individuals, you have taken the time to identify these values. You understand what your money can do for you and how it can help you live a more purposeful and fulfilling life. Just because you aren't taking as many vacations as your sister, investing in a new car, or buying the new tech trend, doesn't mean you aren't making progress.

Creating a Plan That Works for You

Where many people get caught up in the budgeting of their money management is usually where there is often a lot of forecasting. We tend to create a budget based on what we think we will spend or contribute. The problem with forecasting is that it doesn't allow you to honestly look and distribute the money you actually have coming in, to where it will really be going out to.

In an ideal world, we would all love to place $200 or more in our vacation fund a month plus add in an extra $300 for our emergency fund or retirement and then have a good $300 left over to spend on other luxuries and fun things. Most of us do not have that much money to just put aside, especially if you are trying to pay off debt or save up for a huge investment like a new home or car.

You can say you will set aside a certain amount of money for these funds and then after the first month of sticking to your budget be completely disappointed when you cannot contribute as much as you said you would. This goes for categories in your budget you swear you are going to spend less in for instance, groceries. You may only allocate $50 dollars a week to do the family grocery shopping but as much as you try to keep in under that $50, you go over. You then attach a great deal of guilt and shame to having spent more just on buying food your family needs to live on.

Thus, it begins the endless disappointment and guilt of creating a forecasted budget. You don't have to fall into this trap. You have already tracked where your money is going, how much you have coming in and have identified your shopping triggers. You already know what you tend to spend too much money on, and you already set up new habits to help you stay on track with your budget.

Meanwhile, even with all this information, you are probably still looking at the numbers thinking there is no way you can make your financial goals work. Before you get discouraged and give up, let's walk through the process of creating a budget that will actually work for you. You can learn how to properly balance what you save and what you spend so you can not only achieve those financial goals but feel more confident about setting even bigger ones!

How to set up a budget?

Your budget will breakdown to include the following items Provide a sample break down of expenses:

1. What you are obligated to pay monthly

2. Bills that don't occur monthly but that you can break up into smaller monthly payments, so they are not a big hit all at once.

3. Emergency fund

4. Savings

5. Priorities (what you want to spend your money on and what else you want your money to do for you).

While most of these are self-explanatory it is important that you be specific about exactly where your money goes. Know exactly which bills and debts your money is going to and what activities or fun accounts you want to include in your budget.

When sitting down to create your accounts and determine how much you should be adding to each account keep the following in mind.

1. Forget forecasting.

Forecasting is when we focus on money that should be coming our way such as future paychecks or tax returns. You only focus on the money you have right now when you create your budget. Don't think about the money that will come in in a few days when you get paid. Get out of the habit of focusing on future money. When you only focus on what you have you will begin to realize and shift your mindset into taking action to reach your financial goals.

2. *Don't quit on the first round.*

When you are new to budgeting it is common to feel discouraged your first round. This is normal and expected. When you only focus on creating a budget around the money you have on hand you will feel a little on edge that you just don't have enough to do all the things you want. This can take some fine-tuning. You may be able to still fit in all the things you want and you may need to cut back on how much you spend doing those things.

3. *Prioritize.*

You have to be clear about what and when you will spend your money. At first, this seems as an endless waiting game and doesn't add up to much fun unless you are willing to get creative and make it fun. Prioritizing where your money goes helps you reach the goals you said you would reach. Focusing on the money you have on hand helps you easily identify where you prioritize. You can easily cut out hundreds spending on things that would be nice but aren't as important as reaching your financial goals. It is a trade-off between what do you want now versus what do you want most.

4. *Always keep in mind what your money is doing for you.*

This simple way of looking at money as opposed to what I can afford or what I should spend my money on can make all the difference in your spending habits. You are simply being more cautious about your money. You are deciding where and what you will spend your money on and do so with confidence. You won't have to feel shame or guilt about purchasing those new shoes or morning coffee. You will have already decided that these are things you want to spend your money on and they don't interfere with you meeting your bigger financial goals. You decide what gets paid and how much and this provides you with an amazing amount of freedom.

5. *Tap into how you feel.*

One of the best ways to determine what you should be setting money aside for can be best done if you focus on how you feel when you suddenly have to come up with a few extra hundred dollars to cover a necessary bill. If you feel uneasy, stressed, anxious, or guilty about what you spend your money on, then there is a good reason that you either need to be saving for these expenses more or you need to be cutting them from your budget.

Things you want to save for are the things that make you feel stressed or anxious. This is probably how most of us feel when we suddenly see the car insurance bill come in or the water bill landing in our mailbox every couple of months. We can eliminate this stress and anxiety by setting aside a small amount each month so that when the bill arrives it is not such a big shock or surprise.

When you feel guilty or uneasy about the money you are spending ,this could be a good indication that you might want to be cutting back on your spending in this category. Spending your hard-earned money should make you feel good and proud. If you are deciding whether or not you should make a purchase and don't get a good feeling about going through with it, then walk away from it. This can be a red flag that you are making this purchase for hidden reasons often to cover up an emotion you don't want to confront or that the purchase doesn't align with what you truly value.

Finding a Balance Between Saving and Spending

There is a common rule that many financial advisors tend to claim is the best way to budget one's money. For most, this breaks down to 50% of your income should go to your obligations such as housing bills and food, 20% should go to savings, and 30% should go towards non-essential or fun. This seems idealistic and simple. But we all don't make the same amount, some of us have more debt to pay off, and those with kids need to consider savings not just for themselves but for college funds and additional emergencies that occur when you have kids. Breaking your income up into this simplistic formula may be a great starting point but is often not realistic for many.

Striking a balance between spending and savings doesn't have to be a challenge and it does not have to be restrictive. When you want to determine how much you have to save and spend you need to first ensure you have the essentials covered. All the bills you need to pay each month that are necessary for you to survive, will fall into your essential or your obligation. Some things like your phone bill, cable bill, and minimal credit card payments may also be included in these essentials. Although you may find that you can make some cuts to these types of essentials if needed.

Add up all the essentials and subtract this amount from your monthly income. Keep in mind, some of these essentials will not be the full balance. For bills that you know you can expect at some point in the year, you will want to divide up into equal monthly payments so that when the bill comes you have it covered and you aren't scraping together the money when the bill comes in. Once you know how much your essentials will cost you, you can calculate what percentage of your income needs to go to your obligation each month.

Once you have subtracted your essentials from your income, the money you have left over is what you can spend or save. Before you start splitting up this leftover income or feel discouraged about the amount, take the time to write the things you want. The main reason people get discouraged living on a budget is that they neglect having money for the things they want. Budgeting without having money to spend on the things that you want, defeats the whole purpose of a budget. Your budget shouldn't make you feel as though you are missing out on the good things that bring you joy. However, you need to know exactly what these wants are.

Wants are the things you don't need to survive but they bring you joy and you like the idea of having the money to indulge a little on these things. Some examples include:

- Eating out
- Going to the movies
- Designer shoes or clothes
- Gourmet coffee
- New tech gadgets

Don't fret about funding these just yet but be clear about the things that you would really feel you were depriving yourself of in case you didn't get to enjoy them regularly. You will quickly learn that it is possible to be able to enjoy the things you love and work towards more of the things that will bring you success in life.

On to the savings side. You won't know how much you need to set aside for saving if you don't know what you are saving for. Whether it is to build up an emergency fund or to start putting some money aside for retirement. You need to have a goal to be working towards. If we want to reach the goal of being able to set 20% of our income aside as typically suggested, this can be a starting point, but start with just 10% if 20% seems to be overwhelming. Once you get comfortable with saving 10% you can bump up to 15% a month. As you continue to evaluate your budget, you will find it easier to make the necessary changes to the budget that will allow you to reach your savings goals. Or just setting a realistic goal of $50 or $100 dollars a month to get you started.

So, now you know what percentage of your income goes to the obligations and you have a goal of saving 10% of your income, the percentage you have left over goes toward your wants. Now you can begin to allocate your spending money where you want it to go. Some of this spending money you may decide can go into a savings account to fund future wants such as a vacation or higher-priced items. Having a guilt-free spending account is what will allow you to benefit from financial freedom. When you have your needs covered, your savings being added to, you can enjoy what is left over.

While you may have bigger financial goals that make you feel like you need to cut out all non-essential spending to fund your future goals, this is the mentality many get trapped into. They think if they just save everything now, they will feel more financially secure and stress less. Nonetheless, not enjoying even a little of your hard-earned cash now will quickly lead to resentment and you will easily fall into the mindset of "budgeting isn't for me". Allow yourself some of what you want now.

Chapter 6: It Is Time to Escape Your Debt

When you have a budget that is working for you, you will be able to pay off your debt with less stress. Debt is not easy to avoid. We all have some amount of debt we are hoping to pay off as quickly as possible and some of us are completely unaware of how certain debts are keeping us stuck in our money problems. Not all debt is bad. You need to show lenders that you are able to pay back money you borrow responsibly and the only way to prove this is if you have some kind of debt that you are actively paying back.

What we often neglect to understand is that certain debts will keep you stuck in financial strain indefinitely if you don't make the commitment to pay them off.

Types of Debt

There are a number of different types of debt we accumulate over our lifetime. We can most of the time not avoid having a small amount of debt attached to our name but many of us have a great deal of debt that is causing us to stay stuck in our money struggles. While some debt can be beneficial others are just damaging if not paid off in full as soon as you acquire them. These types of destructive debts are what keep us paying more than we have on things we could do without or at least waited to purchase.

Secured debt

Secured debts are those that allow you to borrow a

certain amount of money under the stipulation that an asset is underlying if you are unable to pay back the loan. A car loan is the perfect example of this type of debt. You get approved for a certain amount of cash to pay for a new car, the purchased car is the lien. If you are unable to make the payments on the loan, then the car can be repossessed and sold to cover what you haven't paid. These loans are fairly straightforward and have low to moderate interest rates.

Unsecured debt

Unsecured loans are those that are offered in good faith alone. You do not need to put anything up for lien or as collateral to receive this type of loan. If you do fail to make the repayments the lender can sue you, which is never an ideal option as this is quite costly. Instead, lenders tend to add on a high-interest rate for unsecured loans. Medical bills, membership contracts for a gym or country club, and credit cards are some examples of unsecured debt that you can incur.

Revolving debt

Revolving debt refers to a set money limit that a borrower can use on a recurring basis. They can be in the form of a credit card or a line of credit. The borrower is expected to pay a minimal amount each month based on how much of the credit limit they have spent. Revolving debt can be a secured or unsecured debt so you can have a low or a high-interest rate.

Mortgages

Mortgages are long-term large sum loans. They are taken out to purchase a new home and are a type of secured debt where the purchase property is the collateral. These loans tend to have a relatively low-interest rate and tend to have a repayment plan that lasts from 15 to 30 years

The number one debt that will keep you from your financial goals is credit card debt. This is a revolving debt which allows you to spend money you don't have each month even without having to pay to make what you already owe. The problem is most credit cards are unsecured so they come with a fairly high-interest rate, meaning you will end up owing far more the longer you allow for this debt to sit around unpaid.

The Effects of Credit Card Debt

Most of us have grown up with the thinking that whatever money we don't have we can easily cover by using a credit card. This buy now pay later option, has caused many to accumulate thousands of dollars in debt. Credit cards have allowed millions to live beyond their means.

You may be making the minimum payments each month but often if your credit limit is high and you have maxed out that limit, your monthly payments are barely covering the interest rates, so your bill only goes down a few dollars each month. Not being able to pay off your balance at the end of the month results in you having to pay more than what you originally did for what you purchased. These interest rates can change at any time as well. You may sign up for a card that offers a low-interest rate but after a few months, this interest rate can significantly increase. If you have a balance left on your card this balance gets hit with that higher interest rate and you get further behind.

It is incredibly enticing to buy now and worry about paying later. The instant gratification you get from being able to buy when you don't have the money can ruin your credit and keep you stuck in financial strain. The less you are able to pay on your balance each month the more you will end up paying. Since your interest rates will then be added to your remaining balance, this then gets charged the interest rate. You end up paying interest on your interests. This is why it takes so many of us a much longer time to pay off our credit card debt and in the end, we end up spending much more than we intended. All because of the instant gratification of being able to buy now.

Credit cards are an attractive way to spend money you don't have. As long as you pay the minimum balance each month you can spend until you reach the limit. The problem is that most of us spend the maximum limit without having the minimum payment on hand. This causes us to incur more debt and penalty fees that dig us deeper into debt. As mentioned, the interest you get charged on your remaining balance carries over each month.

These cards aren't just enticing because they allow you to make purchases now and pay for it later, many stores and card companies have special offers or discounts that make us believe we are getting our money's worth. You might have signed up because a store or company gave you a huge discount on your first purchases or gave you a number of months where you didn't have to worry about paying interest on your balance. These seem like smart spending choices. You get your first purchase for less than you intended to pay and then you don't have to worry about paying interest while you are paying off your balance. What ends up happening is when we don't have to worry about the interest, we tend to neglect to pay off the balance before the end of the no-interest time frame. By the time we realize we need to pay off the remaining balance, without getting hit with a high-interest rate, we don't have a plan in place to pay off the debt.

Not all credit cards are the same either. Many store retail cards tack on a much higher interest rate, but these cards can be easier to get for someone with a lower credit score. These types of cards also add on reward incentives to get people to use their cards more often. Some of these retail cards may have their logo on them but they partner with a credit company that allows you to use this card anywhere, not only in the store. The Amazon card is a prime example of this.

Paying Off Debt

Begin by first creating a spreadsheet that allows you to see how much credit card debt you actually have. You want to list all the credits you have and what the remaining balance is on each of them . Also, write what the current interest rate is on each of the cards.

Once you have a clear vision of what your credit card debt looks like, there are two ways you can approach getting yourself out of credit card debt.

1. Pay off the smaller debts

With this first approach to paying off your debt, you will rank them from the highest balance to the lowest. If you have done your financial confidence builder from Chapter 2, you already know it is possible to eliminate one small debt quickly. Building off this exercise, you can begin to pay off each smaller debt first. This is a simple three-step process.

Step one: Organize debt from smallest to largest amounts.

Step two: Pay the minimum on larger debts, pay more than the minimum on the smallest debt.

Step three: Once the smallest debt is paid off, put that money towards the next biggest debt.

2. Pay the highest interest rates

Sometimes, paying the smaller debts means your bigger debts are going to grow much larger depending on the interest rates. If you have a debt or multiple debts that have significantly higher interest rates it might be wiser to pay these off first. This can be hard as you need to pay more than what the interest rate adds on plus enough to bring the balance down.

Step one: Organize your debt according to their interest rates with the highest being at the top and the lowest rates at the bottom.

Step two: Calculate how much you need to pay on the highest interest rate in order to cover the interest and bring down the monthly balance.

Step three: Pay on the highest rate debt until paid off in full. Then move the money you were paying on the first debt to the net highest rate.

Neither of these debt pay-off approaches are ideal. What is even more beneficial is that you won't have to recalculate how much money you allocate to debt pay-off. You already start with a set amount that you will pay each month and you just continue with this amount, moving more of it to the next debt each time you pay-off one. This allows you to quickly eliminate debt from your budget. Once that first debt is paid off, the others go down substantially since you have additional money being dispersed to the next debt.

Another option that you can look into is consolidating your debt to one card that offers a low-interest rate. This is not always the most effective way to pay off debt, especially if you haven't gotten into a good flow with sticking to a budget. You may find yourself constantly moving your debt from one low-interest rate to another, never actually addressing the issue or taking action to pay it off. Consequently, this can make it more feasible for you to pay off your debt by only having to worry about paying one account instead of multiple ones.

Chapter 7: Dealing With Your Budget

When you first set out to stick to a budget, it is important to review your budget monthly. This will help you quickly identify what is and is not working. Monthly reviews of your budget will ensure that you stay on track with your financial goals and will allow you to continuously make progress to not only gain control of your money but will also allow you to live life according to your terms, not how much money you have.

Things to Keep in Mind When Reviewing your Budget:

1. What categories are you spending less than you had budgeted for?

2. What categories are you spending more than you had budgeted for?

3. Has anything changed that will affect your budget?

4. What is the number one thing you want your money to be doing for you?

5. What is making it more challenging for you to stick with your budget?

Reflecting on Your Budget

Once you have gotten into a smooth routine with your monthly budget, it can be easy for anyone to simply stick with it. While this can help you maintain a secure financial situation, it doesn't necessarily help reach the goals set. In order to ensure we stay on track with our financial goals, we need to make time to regularly reflect on the budget we create. A budget is never a fixed and permanent plan. We all desire new things and may find that more important things have come about that will require us to shift where our money goes.

In order to avoid falling into budgeting traps as you gain control over your money, your budget needs to be reviewed regularly. Even if you are satisfied with your money situation, reviewing your budget can help you see if there are areas in your life that you want to put more money towards or have realized that certain areas don't require as much. As you grow and your life changes, your budget will also need to change and hopefully grow with you.

When you sit down to review your budget, the first thing you want to look over are the financial goals you set. By reviewing these first, you will be able to stay focused on the purpose your budget is supposed to serve. After reviewing your goals, ask yourself if these goals are still relevant. When you first start budgeting, your goal may have been to pay off a specific debt, and through the process of sticking with your budget you have been able to accomplish this in a short amount of time. Maybe your goal was to have an emergency fund set aside which you have accomplished. If you have already met some of your financial goals, they are no longer relevant. This is a good way to identify areas where you can shift your money from one category to another or create a whole new category to fund.

As you review your budget keep in mind those financial goals that are no longer relevant. Also, keep in mind the goals you haven't reached yet. Remember to track the progress you are making toward those unmet goals. Ask yourself and answer the following questions honestly.

- What is working with your budget?

- How has it improved your life?

- Are there things that are too tight or loose with your finances that you need to adjust?

- Are you spending more on the things that really matter to you?

No-Spend Challenge

Setting up a budget allows you to recognize where you are spending money that you don't need to spend. One way you can increase your savings and cut back on spending on non-essentials is through a no-spend challenge. A no-spend challenge requires you to be more disciplined about what you spend your money on. It is an ideal time to cut back on spending especially after the holiday season or after taking a vacation. This time period helps you get back on track after either spending more or having to rest your budget from an unexpected financial hit.

Why commit to a no-spend challenge?

Going a period of time without spending helps you reset after a slip-up. We all can get off track, but we don't have to stay off track. A no-spend challenge is an easy way to get back on track.

A no-spend challenge can give your savings a boost. When you are making the conscious effort to spend less, you can put more towards your emergency fund, vacation fund, or towards your financial goals.

You will notice where you can cut back on spending in your regular routines. You may have given yourself a substantial fund for things like groceries, gas, or eating out, but after a no-spend challenge, you may see that you don't need to give yourself that big of an allowance.

No spending challenges are short time periods, so you don't have to worry about feeling deprived for a lengthy time. Unlike when you need to cut back on spending because you need to pay for other obligations, a no-spend challenge occurs on your own terms. This can help you feel more confident and in control of your money. No spending challenges can be as short as a weekend or as long as a month. How long you decide to commit to a no-spend challenge is up to you! The key is that once you say you are going to do it, you stick with it. If you want to go for a week then don't decide after two days that you have had enough. Stick with it and you will reap the rewards.

Weekend No-Spend Challenge

A no-spend weekend challenge is a fun way to see how you can get creative with doing more things at home or for free. If you have kids, this might seem like a daunting challenge. How can you possibly keep the kids entertained without spending money? In fact, this is actually a great time you can get in some quality bonding time with your children and it also can help them see that there is more to having fun than spending a fortune.

For those with kids, you have a number of resources you can tap into that will help you find free activities and events around your community to take part of. Often your local children's museum, local zoo, and science center will have free activities throughout the year. Some other ideas can include:

- Hiking
- Picnic in the park
- Popcorn and movie night at home
- Going for a bike ride
- Game night
- A scavenger hunt around the community

For couples looking for some free activities to do together can include:

- Cooking a meal together
- Going for a walk
- Reading a book together

- Building a puzzle

- Checking off one of your DIY projects together.

- Organizing the house, spring cleaning, or rearranging the family room

If you are solo, there are plenty of things you can find to keep yourself busy without having to go out and spend.

- Start a new hobby

- Set life goals

- Host a small get together at your place and ask everyone to bring their favorite appetizers

A weekend no spend challenge can help you get back on track with your budget quickly. You can easily save an extra hundred dollars or more.

Week-Long No-Spend Challenge

A week-long challenge will allow you to focus on your daily spending habits. You will spend less on those morning coffees or grabbing lunch out. Instead, you'll prep your lunches for work, set your coffee pot to go off in the morning so you have it ready to pour and go, and you can make changes in your commute. Instead of driving everywhere you find ways to walk or ride your bike to save on gas. Instead of cooking a meal every night you will get creative on how to use leftovers instead of throwing away food at the end of the week.

This challenge will bring more awareness on what you can comfortably cut out of your daily spending whether it is just for a week or make it a permanent effort so you can put your money towards more of the things that matter most to you.

A week-long no spend challenge will allow you to boost your savings. With this challenge, you can easily save a few hundred dollars when you keep your financial goals in mind. This challenge is especially helpful after you have taken an unexpected financial hit or after enjoying a vacation. This challenge will allow you to quickly restock your savings or have more money on hand to pay for financial obligations you are worried about coming up a little short on.

Month-Long No-Spend Challenge.

The month-long challenge is one that can help you establish better money management for the long term. Although it is not always easy at first as most of us tend to focus on what we can't spend money on, making a shift in your mindset will allow you to tackle this challenge with ease and enthusiasm. A month-long no-spend challenge will allow you to better adapt to more healthy spending habits. Maybe you want to cut back on impulse buying, make better use of your grocery money, or lower your spending on non-essential items.

A month-long challenge is one you undertake when you want to seriously master your spending habits. It is about making permanent changes to how you use your money and making your money work for you in ways that will allow you to live the life you dream of.

Unlike with weekend or week-long no-spend challenges, the habits you adhere to during a month-long no spend challenge are more likely to stick and be ones you commit to even after the month-long challenge has ended.

Through a month-long challenge, you will identify where you are unnecessarily spending money. It also helps you better plan your month and not get caught up in spending money you know you want to be using for more important wants.

Keep in mind that with any no spending challenge, it is not a way for you to spend less one week so you can spend more the next. These challenges are meant to help you reach the financial goals you have established. Once you have finished your no-spend challenge you shouldn't fall into the mindset that, since you spent less during the challenge you now have more to spend after the challenge. The no-spend challenge is to help fund your long-term goals and you don't want to fall back into instant gratification by spending what you just saved immediately.

Simple rules of a no-spend challenge

1. **Only spend on what you need**. Whether it is for the weekend or a month you will significantly cut back on what you spend on. Keep in mind this isn't forever so if you find yourself feeling like you are struggling because you aren't enjoying all the things you used to spend your money on before, this is only

temporary. You can easily find other ways to enjoy things that won't cost you money.

2. **Stock up before you start.** Before committing to a non-spend challenge, it is best to stock up on your household essentials before you begin. Things such as laundry detergent, dog food, self-care items, and other essentials can dip into your spending budget. Since this is a time period where you want to spend as little as possible, try to have as many of these items already stocked up.

3. **Cut back or eliminate spending on wants.** During a no-spend challenge you will skip out on the gourmet coffees, stores sales, and other wants. If you fear you won't be able to resist the temptation, then have a plan in place to avoid your spending triggers. Make your coffee at home and take it with you, find a way to avoid the stores you love the most and stick with the bare minimum.

4. **Keep your goals in mind.** Many people struggle with a no-spend challenge because they focus on everything they are not spending on. If you keep your financial goals in mind, you won't stress or feel deprived about skipping on the wants for a short time. Having a visual handy or reminder of what you are giving up this weekend, week, or month for in the long run.

5. **Get everyone in your household involved.** When others depend on you for

their survival or you have a spouse who you share expenses with, you need to have everyone in the house on the same page. Including everyone else in the no-spend challenge can make it more fun and they can help with coming up with free activities.

6. **Avoid temptations**. Don't leave the house with your bank or credit card on you. If you know you have an easy way to say yes to spending while you are out, you will be more likely to cave into spending. It is much easier to say, "no." when you do not actually have the money on you.

7. **Stay busy.** Boredom is a common trigger for many to begin spending. To eliminate this trigger, try to keep yourself busy with things you enjoy and things that you have been wanting to get done but haven't gotten to yet. Staying busy will make the time fly by as well.

8. **Keep a list of things you feel the urge to buy instead of actually buying them**. This list can be used to set your financial goals. Else, revisit in a few days to see how much you don't actually want or need these items.

9. **Set the money you save from your no-spend challenge aside.** Know where the money you are saving is going to go. You want to have a designated account for your no-spend savings in place. Will you be putting this money to lower your debt, bulk up your emergency fund, or to pay for other bills that

are coming up. Maybe you are using it to kick start a vacation fund? Wherever the money is going, be sure to know ahead of time, this way you can use this as motivation to not spend during the challenge.

10. **Plan ahead.** Planning ahead on a no-spend challenge is essential for your success. Have a number of free activities to choose from, don't plan for any girls' nights out or birthday parties. Create a low-budget meal plan so you won't have to worry about spending extra on groceries. Nothing that you can plan out. This will make avoiding spending easier and will give you more confidence in following through with it to the end.

Chapter 8: How to Persevere When Things Get Rough

When you become comfortable with your budget, you might lose track of doing regular check-ins, then all of a sudden an unexpected curveball comes flying your way. All of a sudden you feel like you are right back where you started from. You instantly think that this entire budgeting nonsense is not meant to work out for you. Before you lose all hope in your ability to manage your money, remember, one financial hit or even ten does not mean you need to give up.

You started out on this path for a deeply rooted reason. Maybe it was to live debt-free, go back to school, start your own business, or buy your dream home, whatever the reason it is vital that you dig deep and bring that why to the forefront. When you get hit with a huge financial strain out of nowhere, it can be hard to put things into perspective and incredibly easy to get sucked into the overwhelm and dread.

The purpose of your budget, however, has been preparing you for these situations. While they may make a dent in your planning, they shouldn't completely derail your progress. Nevertheless, even if you have some of the expenses covered, it can be pretty discouraging to have to go back and seemingly start all over. Keeping your purpose in mind will allow you to not only overcome the financial setbacks but, it will allow you to rework your budget so you can get back on track and stay ahead of any other unforeseen money problems you may encounter.

Why You Started

When a huge hit comes to your budget it is important to look back on the list of things you will gain by persevering. When you first started out with your budget you should have made a list of how gaining control over your money would improve your overall quality of life. If you haven't made this list, now is the time to do it. List the things you want to see change in your life when you gain control over your finances. The most common changes that can come about when you obtain the financial security you are after include:

- Feeling less stress

- Gaining more confidence

- Living debt free

- Obtaining the things that are important to you

- Setting bigger goals

Now, take a minute to really visualize this list coming to life. The financial goals you have set for yourself are what will get you to make this visualization a reality. How would sticking with your financial goals make you feel when you have accomplished the freedom you are seeking? This feeling is what will make it easier to overcome and twist and turns you may face along the way. Remember, a budget is flexible. When something major changes or happens in your life your budget can change to help you stay in control.

Financial Setbacks

What happens when you get hit with a setback that you did not plan or budget for? There is no way to avoid unexpected financial hits. Things will come up, medical bills, car repairs, new water heater, kids' activities and so on. These sudden financial strains can make you feel as though you will never get ahead or on track with your money management. Meanwhile, by sticking with a budget and setting aside emergency funds, these unfortunate expenses won't derail you.

We cannot properly plan for these setbacks. There is no way of knowing when life is going to hit you with an event that will require a great deal of money to fix or replace. As we have discussed, there are ways you can build up a small emergency fund to cover most of life's unexpected mishaps. The only way you can begin to build up these funds is to create the appropriate categories for them. This takes a great deal of self-control. When you notice you have a good amount of money just sitting around it can be incredibly tempting to make use of that money now. But, if you have been building upon your financial literacy and discipline, you know that leaving these emergency cash stashes alone will be an incredible lifesaver when something that would normally throw you off comes about.

How can you stay ahead or on track?

You should already have an emergency fund in place that can help cover some unexpected costs, yet remember an emergency fund is more for when you are not getting a guaranteed income. This is not a fund you want to tap into when you don't need to. Instead of relying on your emergency fund stash to cover unexpected costs, you can save a little for those unexpected,yet part-of-life events.

Setting up savings for the unexpected financial hits you know may eventually occur, will keep you on budget and actually keep you ahead with your goals. You know that car repairs are bound to come about, you know that there are certain things in your home that will eventually need to be upgraded, replaced, or repaired. You know that it is unlikely that you or your children will never get sick or hurt. By setting a small amount of money aside each month for these emergency situations you won't stress when they come about. No matter how inconvenient or unexpected they may appear to be.

You can create a separate fund for each of these instances and put away a small amount of money each month so that when the unexpected happens you already have it covered. Before you begin thinking you are already putting so much away for savings and now you will have even less to spend, rest assured a small amount like five or ten dollars a month or out of your paycheck will have little effect on you being able to enjoy your money. You are giving yourself the freedom of not stressing when you get a hard hit in life. You don't need to continuously place money into these funds. You can set a savings amount and once you reach that amount you can reallocate that money elsewhere. Maybe you only put $25 a month in your home repair funds until you reach a fixed amount.

Maybe you set aside a few hundred for emergency medical bills. Maybe you decide to set aside just enough to cover half the cost of a major car repair. Setting aside even a little money now will keep you from being completely thrown off when an event does occur.

The fact is that unexpected financial hits may occur unexpectedly, but most are ones that we all experience. We just avoid preparing for them ahead of time. When you have a budget in place that can account for these unexpected hits, they won't feel like big blows to your savings when they occur.

Reworking Your Budget

Your budget is not a static plan. What may be working for you now, may not be ideal for you in the future. As we grow there will be other things that become important to us. Once you start seeing the success you have with sticking to a budget you might just find yourself believing that you can actually accomplish and have more of the things you only used to dream about.

Regardless of the reason, there will be times where it is absolutely necessary for you to review and rework your budget. But this isn't something you just want to do. If your current budget is working for you and nothing big is changing in your life in the near future, there is no legitimate reason to change what is working. If on the other hand, you are expecting a big change like a family addition, moving to a new home (either upsizing or downsizing) kids going away to college, or expected time off from work, you will want to revisit your budget and plan for these changes sooner rather than later.

Avoid the miscellaneous fund

You want to save up for those big financial hits but what about those sudden smaller ones that can end up adding up throughout the month? If you have children you know that there are often unexpected purchases that occur when one of them breaks something, spills something, or has an accident away from home. Or if you don't have kids and you suddenly find yourself in need of a new briefcase for work, running on your lunch break to buy a new button-up shirt because you spilled coffee on the one you are wearing but have an executive meeting you need to attend still. Or what if you simply lost your mascara, tore your contacts, or need to replace your to-go coffee cup? You don't want to just spend what you have if it is meant to be used elsewhere. These little unexpected expenses can cause you to panic and feel as though you have thrown off your entire plan. These little expenses can add up throughout the month.

One thing that most people do is set up a miscellaneous fund. This is often to account for the random unexpected expenses that may occur in the month. Having a fund like this in place so you can quickly buy new contacts when you accidentally lose one or buy a new pair of shoes when your heel breaks is great, but what often occurs is that this just becomes another shopping stash. Soon you are buying a new shirt, haircuts, a manicure, a second coffee trip, and whatever else you suddenly feel like you need. Instead of a miscellaneous fund, organize your expenses in their appropriate category. You can still have a little monthly emergency fund for when your kid decides to experiment on cutting their own hair or their sibling's hair, you can rest assured that you have some money set aside to cover this life's unexpected moments.

When Should You Change Your Budget?

For the first few months of sticking to a budget, you will want it to remain flexible. The first budget you create will most likely not be the one that works best for you. In the first month of your budget, you might realize you completely underestimated how much you would spend on food or gas and will need to increase those allowance. Other non-essentials where you may have overestimated your spending you might realize you can actually cut back on a great deal more. Once you have gone through the trial and error, your budget should then remain fairly similar month-to-month. And the changes you make will most likely be minor to help pay for short-term goals like a weekend getaway, birthday party, or family visit.

When a major life event occurs, however, your budget will need to be reworked. The most common big life events that will require you to revisit and make bigger adjustments to your budget include:

1. *Getting married.*

Getting married is one of those big milestones many get swept up in. Planning a wedding and paying for a wedding is a huge financial strain whether you are paying for the wedding or not. Young couples are especially vulnerable to getting caught up in planning their dream wedding where money is of no concern.

Even after the marriage, there are a number of other budgeting changes that you will now have to accommodate. Firstly, the budget you create is not just yours. You now have your spouse to consider. However, the way you decide to split up the monthly and yearly expenses is up to the two of you, but you will need to sit down and establish your financial goals together.

If you have been wanting to make a big career change and start your own business, you and your spouse need to come up with an appropriate budget that will allow for that to happen.

What about living arrangements? You may or may not have been sharing living spaces already with your spouse but is this just a temporary arrangement? Do you have plans to move into a bigger home? How will a move affect your commute? Will you need to shell out more for gas or will you be able to bike to work more often and save in that area? What will the new taxes look like?

Marriage is a beautiful new adventure and it is one you take with a loving partner. Most couples put off talking about their finances until it becomes a major issue in their marriage. One of the leading causes for divorce is due to financial strain. The sooner you and your partner sit down and discuss your finances openly and honestly, the better. If one of you has a substantial amount of debt before getting married, you might want to hold off on paying for a wedding until this debt is eliminated or at least at a more manageable amount. Many couples find that having a modest wedding better fits with their financial goals so they can more easily pass up the extra expenses that quickly add up to tens of thousands of dollars.

When you sit down to talk about a budget together you both should bring your goals to the table. This way you can create a budget that will allow both of you to work towards accomplishing what you truly want. This may not be a quick process, planning out the future of your lives together can take some time, but you can both begin to make the necessary changes or begin tracking your expenses so you can have a much clearer view of where you are at and the steps you need to take to get to where you both want to go.

2. *Having a baby.*

A baby is a wonderful life event but with the beauty of becoming a parent there comes a great deal more you need to plan and budget for. Will an additional family member mean you need to make a move into a newer home than you were actually planning for? Can you manage in a smaller space for the first few years? What about the necessities of clothing, diapers, wipes, formula, bottles, and the monthly doctor visits?

Having a baby can quickly eat away a significant amount of your budget.

Once the necessities are taken care of you, also need to consider childcare. If you are married will one of the parents be staying home to take on the role of full-time caretaker or will you both need to be working? If you are both working how will you cover childcare costs? If only one of you is working will that income alone be able to cover all the expenses each month?

There are a number of big items you will need to purchase for your little one as well. A crib, car seat, feeding chair, stroller, and of course items to keep the little one occupied can all cost hundreds of dollars. You'll need to work all these items into your budget before the baby arrives so that you can begin to make the necessary purchases, so you are ready to bring him or her home.

You'll need to do your research before making any purchases to ensure you are getting the best price for each item. You will also want to compare prices on the daily essentials like diapers and wipes so you can properly include these items into your essentials for your monthly expenses.

While having a baby is a joyous occasion to celebrate, understand that they can also bring a great deal of stress into your life if you do not begin to plan for their arrival now.

3. Change in income.

Whether you are making more or making less, any change in income will require you to rework your budget. Those who are blessed to be making more will rework their budget to help them reach their goals in a shorter amount of time. What one should be cautious of is falling into the thought process that having more money means you can spend more.

While you may be able to add to your fun money account you don't want to neglect adding to your savings and goals accounts. The easiest way to get off track when you are making more money is thinking you don't have to put as much importance on paying things the way you were when you had a lower income.

Those who are hit with an income cut will need to reevaluate what they are spending their money on. You will begin to find better ways to save with the non-essential items while still having the money to cover your obligations and find some fun.

4. Career change.

A career change can result in a number of changes that can affect your budget. Maybe there is a change in your income, you might have to travel further or less for work, you might be required to work longer hours or maybe you are working from home. There are many factors that can cause you to make adjustments to your budget. Some areas you might be able to cut back on and therefore put more towards your financial goals. Maybe you will need to add more to certain categories and therefore will need to cut back a little from your non-essentials.

5. *Divorce.*

It is unfortunate when you have to face a divorce, and the last thing you probably want to deal with on top of the other legal matters is your budget. Nevertheless, when you are going from either living off a two-income household to one, or you weren't working and now you will need to find work, your budget should be a top priority. Dealing with a divorce will add unexpected expenses such as lawyer cost and possibly other financial obligations that occur because of the separation. A divorce will cause you to completely restart on a budget of your own. You may have some of the same financial goals as you had when you were married but now you are going to have the satisfaction of reaching those goals on your own. A divorce can be a scary and unstable time financially, but it can also bring a whole new set of opportunities.

Budgeting Goals

Remember, the goal of a budget is to help you enjoy life more. While many of us run at the thought of adhering to a budget, the beauty of it is that you set the rules for your own budget. When you go through the process of truly uncovering what matters most to you, you won't shudder at the thought of a budget but instead, will look at it as another tool to get you to the life you want and deserve to be living.

Many of us tend to give up on a budget when we don't immediately see the rewards we want to be gaining. If you don't see the improvement you want, it is time to look over your budget again.

- Where is your money going?

- What changes can you make?

- Are you being honest?

Many times, a simple change in how you save your money can move you closer to your goals. For many of us having a separate bank account specifically for savings can keep us from unintentionally spending that money. If you notice you tend to dip into your savings with the idea of putting the money back in with your next paycheck, it might be time to set up a separate account.

A budget is meant to work for you. It is meant to help you bring to life your dreams. While you can't expect this to happen overnight, if you are not seeing progress then this calls for you to reevaluate your spending and savings. Are you truly using your money for the things that bring you ultimate joy or are you using it to just feel the instant gratification? Are you putting it away to be financially free or are you keeping yourself stuck by a limiting belief system and unclear values? There are a number of things that can affect your progress, and many can be easily changed but you need to be honest and have the discipline to make the changes if you truly want to gain control over your financial situation.

When a budget isn't working for you, sit down and go over all your goals again. Are they really what you want to achieve or are they things you think you need to achieve because your family is pressuring you or you feel like you are lacking because someone else has more? A budget is meant to cater to your life, and you get to determine how that life is lived.

Conclusion

We are not meant to simply have a job just to pay the bills. We are not meant to stress over working long hours and never enjoy the rewards of our hard work. Life is not meant to be filled with stress, anxiety, and disappointment. Although these are all natural occurrences, your money should not be the root cause for the discomfort you feel in life.

Budgeting is not a quick fix to eliminate this stress and anxiety. Instead, it is a lifelong commitment that will allow you to live more. When you don't have the constant fear of when the next paycheck comes, when you make the effort to get rid of the debt, and you see your savings grow over time, these are the things that make you feel empowered, motivated, and confident.

Many of us have lived with the limiting beliefs that we will never have enough, we will never see our money troubles turn around, and that we will never have that dream life. We may have tried to stick to a budget before never fully grasping what it entails. We set up all our monthly bills to be paid but then neglect to fund our future goals. We quickly become jaded when we get hit with a major financial strain and lose hope.

We fail to address the mindset we have or build the understanding around our finances that can propel us forward. But that can all be changed.

This book has opened up a new door for you to truly gain control over your money. It has walked you through all the steps you need to take to not only create a budget but to stick to one that allows you to achieve great success. You have learned how to track your real expenses, make necessary cuts to your spending, keep your values in focus, and create an action plan that aligns with what you really want out of life.

You now have the tools that will prepare you for the unexpected setbacks in life and plan for the bigger dreams. Whether you are fresh out of high school and embarking on your first adventure as an adult. Whether you have just graduated from college and are now swimming in student loans, or just had a baby. Whether you are planning a wedding or planning your retirement. You now have the right tools, techniques, and understanding of the skills you need to manage your money.

You don't have to live paycheck to paycheck. You don't have to let your debt follow you around. You don't have to let a low paying job or poor spending choices keep you stuck. You can get yourself out of your mediocre situation and live a life of financial freedom. It is now up to you, to be honest with yourself.

Has the way you've been handling your money up until now been working for you? Chances are it hasn't but starting today you can change that answer. You can now begin to create a budget that allows your money to work for you. And when you accomplish this first small step you will realize that you can have so much more success. If you haven't started already, now is the best time to do so! Good luck!

References

10 Unexpected Debt Traps – and How to Avoid Them. (n.d.). Retrieved from https://money.usnews.com/money/personal-finance/debt/articles/2018-09-21/10-unexpected-debt-traps-and-how-to-avoid-them

6 Things Your Spending Habits Reveal About You. (2019, April). Retrieved from https://janlbowen.com/6-things-your-budget-reveals-about-your-life/

Anat, B. (n.d.). Budgeting, But Make It Fun: How One Financial Expert Stays On Track. Retrieved from https://refinery29.com/en-us/how-to-make-budgeting-fun

AnnieReporter. (2018, November). Retail store cards come with perks. Here's the catch . Retrieved from https://www.cnbc.com/2018/11/15/these-credit-cards-can-keep-you-in-debt-longer.html

Berger, S., & Perez, L. (2020, February). Survey: 53% of Americans Live Paycheck to Paycheck. Retrieved from https://www.magnifymoney.com/blog/news/paycheck-survey/

Caldwell, M. (2019, November 20). 7 Why You Should Budget Your Money. Retrieved from https://www.thebalance.com/reasons-to-budget-money-2385699

How to Create Better Spending Habits. (n.d.). Retrieved from https://www.everydollar.com/blog/create-better-spending-habits

Marquit, M. (2019, March 25). How an Attitude of Gratitude Can Help Your Finances. Retrieved from https://www.thebalance.com/how-gratitude-can-help-your-finances-4164181

Mecham, J. (2018). You Need A Budget: the proven system for breaking the paycheck-to-paycheck cycle, getting out of debt, and living the life you. Place of publication not identified: HARPERCOLLINS.

Ramsey Solutions. (2018, December 1). 4 Spending Habits We All Need to Break. Retrieved from https://www.daveramsey.com/blog/money-habits-we-need-to-break

Ramsey Solutions. (2018, November 24). 10 Budgeting Myths You May Be Falling For. Retrieved from https://www.daveramsey.com/blog/budgeting-myths

Ramsey Solutions. (2019, September 13). What Do You Need to Know About Financial Literacy? Retrieved from https://www.daveramsey.com/blog/what-is-financial-literacy

Tana. (2020, February 6). 10 Simple Rules for a No Spend Challenge. Retrieved from https://debtfreeforties.com/budgeting-tips/10-simple-rules-no-spend-challenge/

Printed in the USA
CPSIA information can be obtained
at www.ICGtesting.com
LVHW091314131223
766027LV00069B/2115